The Healing Muse

A Journal of Literary and Visual Arts

The Healing Muse is SUNY Upstate Medical University's journal of literary and visual arts published annually by the Center for Bioethics and Humanities.

The Center for Bioethics and Humanities at SUNY Upstate, established through the generous support of the Medical Alumni Association, is committed to promoting health care which is patient-centered, compassionate, and just. We accomplish this through educational initiatives in bioethics and the medical humanities, clinical ethics consultation, multidisciplinary research and scholarly writing, and health policy analysis and advocacy.

Cover photograph taken by Deborah Rexine
St. Agnes Cemetery, Syracuse, NY

ISSN 1539-6983
ISBN 0-9789605-1-3

The Healing Muse

A Journal of Literary and Visual Arts

Table of Contents

Non-Fiction

Fiction

Visuals

Founding Editor

"Where I live is always a May morning."
from *Passive Resistance* in *Chaminade Literary Review*
B.A. St. Andrews
(1945-2003)

On the Perfect Child

B.A. St. Andrews

Amniocentesis, sonogram, the genomic
road map are all different ways
medicine has planned to cut out difference.

We help parents find their way past Scylla
and Charybdis, past the surprises of
conception now we no longer trust Mother

Nature.
The assurance of prediction,

the perfectibility of man.
What have we prepared for
the changeling child who climbs
a different set of spiral stairs,
this visitor whose XXY suggests
an algebra of aberration, whose
extra chromosome (that embarrassment
of riches) creates an alchemy
of disaster? Our brave new
world has little room for this
fetus and welcomes it with
lullabies like sirens wailing
and the sterile inhalation
of vacuum pumps. A little
act of love gone wrong is
quietly entombed, a tidy
clean-up of the family genome
is achieved and we remove
all trace of this mistake
relieved to welcome the next
perfect child and name it
God made flesh and angel eyes.

Editor's Note

It is with great pride that we present this new issue of *The Healing Muse.* Our writers and visual artists have created another stunning and stimulating collage of human nature: halos, scars, blemishes, the telltale signs of character, chance, and fate. People are often surprising; just when you think you know how someone will behave, he or she veers off in a different direction, dashing your expectations and expanding your sense of possibility.

Illness and suffering would not seem to be a prime location for humor or happiness, yet within these pages and tucked amid a hospital's corridors or a clinic's waiting room they do indeed exist and flourish. Here, physicians and nurses write about their own fears, describe how they see and care for their patients, and delight in the relationships they forge with them. Here, too, those who are experiencing illness describe their lives as comprising so much more than symptoms and suffering, reminding us that we are never merely a diagnosis or a set of statistical probabilities.

In pictures and in words, our artists and writers perform the ancient art of healing by telling the story of how we live and how we die, how we love and how we hate, and how we discover our purpose and our power through such incantation and imagination. Language and art transform and translate the individual's experience into the universal. When we recognize ourselves in the other, we approach the divine. Let *The Muse* show you humanity's endless quest for connection and the compassion such a quest often engenders.

Deirdre Neilen

Vol. 7, No.1 (Fall) 2007

Interview with Rafael Campo

Deirdre Neilen

Rafael Campo teaches and practices general internal medicine at Harvard Medical School and Beth Israel Deaconness Medical Center in Boston. His latest book of poems, The Enemy, *was published in April 2007 by Duke University Press. Our interview took place during a visit he made to Upstate's College of Medicine in April as well as over e-mail. It was quite obvious during his presentations to students and residents that Dr. Campo retains an enthusiasm for his twin professions of medicine and writing that pulls people to him. He seems much more like a newly minted physician than a seasoned veteran of managed care, the AIDS epidemic, and the ongoing nightmare of the medically uninsured. His faith in people and in poetry seems unshaken.*

DN: How do you wake up each day eager to meet the challenges of medicine and compassion?

RC: I've been thinking a lot about this issue as I prepare for a conference addressing the role of the humanities in physician renewal. In my case, I find this renewal in the great imaginative works of art—especially poetry, but also literature in general, and even painting, sculpture, drama, and dance—that address the illness experience.

DN: Yet so many physicians seem burned out and almost disinterested in anything beyond the treatment regimen they're proposing.

RC: I suspect some of the "war weariness" we care providers often come to feel has to do with the relentlessness of the biomedical model's defining our work, through the narrow lens of technology, as a kind of battle. Thus, we expend a lot of energy fighting diseases and resisting exactly what is most healing and humanizing in such difficult interactions with actual people who are suffering: our shared capacity for language and narrative, which in turn abets empathy.

DN: Empathy is often set up as a counterweight to the previously praised "detached concern" for physicians to model.

RC: I've always been skeptical of that oxymoron; detached concern was certainly held out to me as the model when I was a medical student. But if we lose the wellspring of the human voice to lend meaning to our work, we are left with a pile of abstract lab test reports and unending forms requiring CPT codes and NPI numbers.

DN: Some medical students who are doing their rotations in the hospital will tell us that detached concern is still being touted as the correct, professional way to behave with patients.

RC: And that's ironic because such distancing is supposed to protect the physician from emotional exhaustion! But in cutting off our natural human responses to patients, we actually risk becoming unfeeling robots, incapable of receiving the nourishment of soulful connection not just to our patients but to our peers as well. It takes great effort to maintain distance and erect these supposedly impenetrable boundaries between us and our patients. I would say this effort inevitably leads to burnout and cynicism within the profession.

DN: You are someone who seems to recognize and take pleasure in medicine's other aspects, its spiritual side and its mysteries. Does this come from your also being a poet?

RC: I do feel that my twin vocations have much to say to one another, on a daily basis! The ancient Greeks believed poetry and healing to be inextricably interrelated, and in fact, the importance of this relationship was even represented in their theology. I've always felt there was something of the divine in the action of creation (poesis, again going back to the Greeks), and what could be more joyful than communion with the gods?

DN: Do you feel this sense of the divine in medicine with your own patients?

RC: There is a real joy for me in the recognition of our shared humanity. I think we aspire to be better than we are, to transcend our earthly limitations. I'm not talking in the material sense but more about our hopes and dreams. We're part of the larger human family, and we can only be more tolerant and forgiving of the foibles and flaws we see in others if we recognize them in ourselves. My wish to be a more caring and compassionate individual is not limited to my being a physician, but I hope it makes me a better one and a better person.

Ode to the Box of Tissues on My Desk in the Clinic

Rafael Campo

Too small for all that you are asked to wipe
away: the streak of blood the speculum
has left inside the blind girl's thigh as I
removed it hastily; her tears, not black
as night, but just as clear as yours or mine;
the bead of pearly semen I expressed
from the urethra of the older man
whose prostate cancer, not another child,
is what will grow to vex him these next years,
a fate my probing finger had revealed;
and all the tears, of course, the junkie cried
for her lost innocence, the HIV
inscribed upon her hardened veins like blots
of ink from an inexact pen. Too small
to wipe away the make-up covering
the bruises on a woman's face in which
I saw the shape of my own fist; the pus
that spurted out of the infected boils
a schizophrenic prisoner revealed
beneath his arm, secretively, as if
displaying stolen merchandise for sale;
and tears, of course, like theirs, though mine seem less
than what you would expect, you, small and square,
and crumpled in the sweaty palm of care.

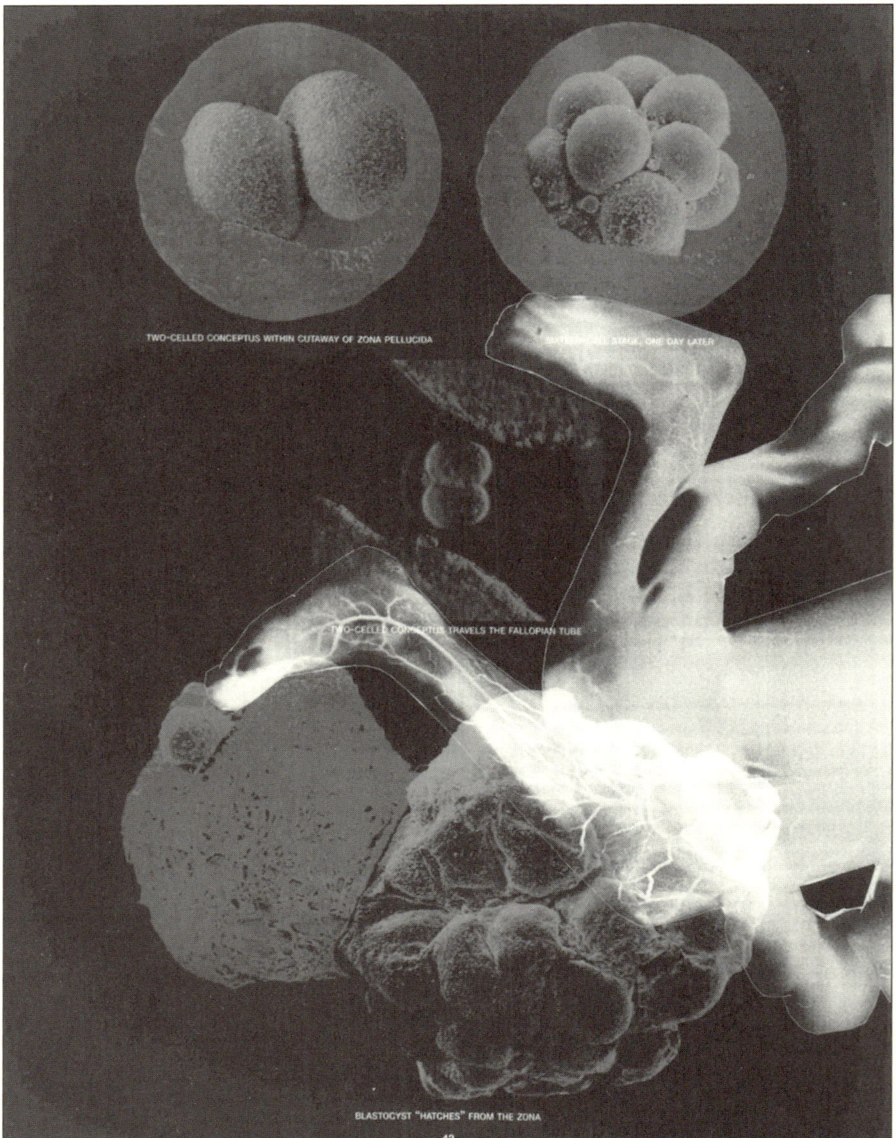

Sarah Nicolai ~ *In Tandem*

Erosion

Bruce Bennett

We see them going, and we let them go.
A word, a glance, a wave; but that is all.
It's time for them to leave us, and we know.

We gather, smile, shake our heads; bestow
a murmured blessing on what must befall.
We see them going, and we let them go.

We've seen the process: how the steady slow
erosion takes them. Seconds seem to crawl.
It's time for them to leave us, and we know

There's nothing, no one, that can halt that flow,
beckon them back, reverse things with a call:
we see them going, and we let them go,

Telling our hearts this oldest tale of woe,
wrapping that grief in comfort, like a shawl.
It's time for them to leave us, and we know

Our time is coming too, and we must show
how we receive what happens to us all.
We see them going, and we let them go.
It's time for us to leave them, and we know.

St. Joseph

Katie Antony

At St. Joseph's they read the "Our Father" every morning at eight, the "Hail Mary" at noon, and they don't do abortions. Otherwise it's a normal hospital where I lie alone waiting to deliver my first baby. I wish the other hospitals weren't full. I haven't done anything the Catholics would consider wrong. I'm married, pregnant, about to deliver, but I feel guilty when other patients or families walk by and see me alone. I want to shout, "My husband is in Iraq," or "He's fighting for your minivans," or even "I'm not totally sure I'm not a widow," but they don't ask, don't stop, and barely glance my way except for a polite smile. Jesus didn't entirely meet his father 'till he died; he was raised by a stepdad. My son won't wait more than six months, I hope—'till Christmas, when he'll be born to his father. Another contraction. They aren't frequent enough. I wonder if my husband is in any pain, a lot of pain, or still able to feel pain, and does he pray over there. Does he pray for his son? His son is late. I don't think he wants to leave—to enter this place, this hospital, this world. A young nun wanders in. Her shoes aren't beige like the other nuns'. She doesn't linger in the doorway but comes straight to my side. Would I like confession? I'm not contracting. I feel a pressure where she never will. I tell her I would; I tell her I've been having bad thoughts. She cups my hands in hers and squeezes. She gently *shhhs*, and we pray for Fathers.

Visit

Katie Antony

An old woman in a hospital bed,
dangling tubes from her mouth and nose,
is turning through tangles to her son.

You have seen how children lean
from their mothers' hands
to reach in vain for elephants at the zoo,
allowing themselves to be pulled back
to their mothers' embrace.

Such is the way this son extends
his arms, then bends away wanting
gravity to pull him, remembering
her weight is not there to anchor him.

She is the creature he beholds.
Behind her bed rails and lines,
her gray face wrinkles with wonder
as she gazes back at her son.

Under a Fearless Sky

Sarah Averill
Dearing Writing Award, First Place
Student Division

You own two shops,
And you run back and forth.
Try to close the one that's a fearful trap,
Getting always smaller. Checkmate,
This way Checkmate that.
Keep open the shop
Where you're not selling fishhooks anymore.
You are the free-swimming fish.
—Rumi

Halfway down the block, the sidewalk turns to a crumbly mixture of asphalt and gravel. A scrap metal truck is parked in front of a clapboard house sided with disintegrating asphalt shingles. The driver of the truck is standing in the wide driveway where once another house stood. Smiling unabashed and toothless, he tells me that when the house was torn down he bought the lot for four hundred dollars. He is gregarious but not imposing; he reminds me of my grandfather who spent most of his life peddling apples. Pointing to the shabby two-story structure behind him, he tells me he has lived in this house for forty years, that the building on the corner used to be a bakery but that the children of the original owners didn't want anything to do with the business, so it had closed.

He offers more: he has a tenant upstairs, a woman with three children who pays him two-fifty a month in rent. She can't afford anything more, he says. I look at the roof, which has been repaired with a variety of materials (roll roofing, shingles of different colors, patches of tar), and wonder if it leaks into the second floor apartment. I dread the thought of the lead paint on the old windows and how it might color the future dreams of the three children living there: make them aggressive, slow their learning, taint their blood. The windows are covered with makeshift curtains. The asphalt shingles on the side of the house are well worn. He says that he is thinking of moving some of the ones from the back to the front to cover up the places where the clapboard is showing. He wants it to look better from the street.

I ask him if anyone uses the park a few doors down from him. "There used to be a house there. Now kids hang out—sell drugs. Once the cops came so fast that no one had a chance to run away, and they bagged them," he grinned as he spoke.

I ask him if he feels safe in the neighborhood. Without hesitating, he says, "Sure, I've been here since before everybody else; no one bothers me." I like him. He is poor, but he has self-confidence that defies anyone to judge his circumstances. He is comfortable and at ease in this place where he makes his home and his living collecting rent and selling scrap metal. Our conversation closes easily, and he turns his attention to his partner; they go back to loading his truck with a defunct furnace. How much for that? I wonder.

I need to walk, especially when my mind is filled up and tired, and my eyes ache from reading for too long. My friends think I've gone mad. They don't understand how I could have left my career as a city planner, age thirty-six, to begin medical school. I explained that I think medicine is too focused on the molecular level and that I could make a difference as a physician focused on the larger picture, especially living conditions. I respect the search for cures, but it is a shame that so little is done to prevent illness. I decided to learn the language of medicine, starting with science. My tongue still trips against my teeth and lips trying to pronounce these foreign words. Medicine has a word for everything. Even for the sound your stomach makes when it's grumbling with hunger. *Borborygmi.* Am I serious? *Borborygmi?* Yes. Try saying it out loud. It could easily be a word from Lewis Carroll's *Jabberwocky.* Delightful. Absurd. Frightening. When I feel discouraged, I go out and walk just to feel my body moving through the dense and palpable world. In full swing every cell in me is jangled to alertness by the rhythm of my movement. My mind responds to the strange beauty it finds, the subtle changes of lighting and color, like the reflection of a tree in a dusty window when the sun breaks through the clouds.

I sometimes walk around places close to my house and sometimes I go across town to less familiar places, where people less privileged than I generally live, packed into a handful of census tracts, along with some frightening statistics. At first I didn't know what guided my exploration or what I hoped to learn. I simply set out on foot with a camera to see this neighborhood at slow speed. I counted as I walked down the block. It takes between five and seven seconds to walk past a house on foot. It takes a minute to walk past twelve houses if you don't stop to look at anything.

I feel out of place, even vulnerable, because I do not live in this neighborhood and have no business here. What if someone doesn't like that I am here? Is this a dangerous place to be? It is cold enough in late October that there aren't many people outside on the street, and mostly I am alone in my meandering walk in the Southwest of Syracuse.

The colors of the paint on some of the houses reflect another era, when houses here were ornately decorated with carefully chosen colors. On this block there is the occasional house with a fresh coat of paint, but mostly the paint is puffed and peeling like a snake shedding its skin. Taken in by the fragments of history, I can overlook the grim reality of this place. This neighborhood is one of the poorest in the city, and its children have the highest incidence of lead poisoning. A couple of times passersby or people sitting on their porches ask me what I am doing. I feel skittish and say something about taking a photography class. I must look as out of place as I feel taking pictures of scenes that are not really remarkable singly but that altogether tell a story about this sliver of human habitat.

There's a house with the windows covered in newspaper. There's another that is covered with splats of paintball paint from the foundation to the third-floor windows. What was going on *that* day? Someone had a wildly fun time aiming and pulling the trigger on that paint-gun, first orange, then dusky blue, then neon green—splat, splat, splat, I can hear the gentle thud as the balls burst on the crusty siding of that once genteel house. Now it looks like a drawing by a third-grader using bingo ink dotters, the kind my grandmother bought when she took me to play on Saturday nights.

Here's one that caught fire. There's another one—who sets the fires? Who watches as they burn? Who puts them out? There's one with the door pried open. I climb the charred stairs and stand in the open doorway. I can see the marbled green linoleum of the kitchen floor in the dim light that slants through the dirty windows. The cupboard hangs open, empty. It is dark inside. I do not go in but wonder who does and what happens there.

There's one house filled with gallon milk jugs; you can see a dozen of those hazy plastic containers pressed against the glass of the mullioned windows. Next comes an abandoned school, with every window broken and every wooden frame warped and threatening to fall. There's a patch of grass between two houses where a house once stood. There's the adult learning center, a low wooden structure with a faded sign. It looks as if it were once a car garage. It's empty now. Grass is coming up through cracks in the swath of pavement out front. The faded green house next to it is boarded up with graying plywood. There's no one here. I stand alone on the sidewalk and contemplate the painfully slow erasure happening here.

This is not my habitat, the discomfort that I feel as I walk down the street tells me. The first time I came over this way, I was pretty nervous, especially when I saw people hanging out on their porches or looking at me as I walked by. Then the second time and the third time I began to feel more comfortable. When the old man told me he felt safe here, it tore another corner from the edge of my fear. Since my conversation with him I have asked other people who live and work near here how they feel about this neighborhood. The ones that live here and work here for the most part don't feel afraid, but they tell stories of other folks not coming.

The director of the Spanish Action League says the other Little League teams won't come to play ball in this neighborhood because someone got shot near the playground last summer. The lifeguard at the Southwest Community Center says not many people come to swim at the pool because of the neighborhood. Her assistant is studying at Bryant and Stratton to be a police officer, but she isn't one yet. She says she feels safe in the neighborhood but doesn't want to be called a cop out in the open for fear of—well, she doesn't know exactly, but just in case.

The landscape, to me, has another kind of warning inscribed in it: Beware of the fire, beware of the flood, beware of the cranes that will come and knock your house down. Beware of the hammers that will board up your windows. Beware of the tricksters in the night that will desecrate your home. Beware of being poor, of a slow and painful erasure. Go and live elsewhere if you can. This place is a big toothless grin—a disappearing act with an invisible magician. A place passing out while waiting to exhale.

Some people live here. Some people feel safe, but I have been warned now not to walk here, especially not alone, especially after dark. I skirt the edges of these warnings. I feel that I too am inching towards invisibility—what do I have that anyone could want: a digital camera, a warm winter coat, the jeans I wear all week and then wash on the weekends. My life in my skin and my camera are the two valuables that I have. The camera I would give up gladly to anyone who asked for it, so I have only my life to lose. No one looks particularly eager to take either. So, why the warnings? Is it really so dangerous, or are the people that warn me, people safely on the other side of this harsh economic and political reality, simply knee-jerk nervous about habitats like this one—that are unfamiliar, that are run down, that don't look safe—to them?

On one corner there is a poorly lit store with no windows; the signs outside advertising sales and services are spray-painted. I consider going in to buy something, but because I can't see inside I hesitate. I feel aversion, anxiety; I don't go in. I am surprised by my reaction. I can't tell what part of this scene evokes such strong feelings. I am not immune to the fear. I scan the landscape with the same trained eye as those who warn me, but I am willing to feel this, the discomfort of being in an unfamiliar place. Again, I have a fish in my stomach. It challenges me to understand what allows places like this to persist and what it would mean to be a doctor here.

Perhaps the warnings are warranted, but I suspect the biggest threat of these places may be something else, something that is not ready to be acknowledged: the sheer fact of their existence in contrast to other places just a few blocks, a mile, two miles, ten miles away. The contrast is what is killing people, and it makes us sick because it isolates and divides us.

The ease with which I can leave this place makes me an outsider. I can come, remark, and go. I am edgy that my good intentions will cause offense, that taking an interest in it might not be enough. The director of the Southwest Community Center said as much of medical students and the medical school. "You folks come around and talk, and then you don't come back," he said. I wonder what might come of my vagabonding about this side of town—loitering, touristing, visiting, and picture-taking. Could I…Might I come for an extended stay? I have not tested the depth of my commitment. There are other languages to learn. I stumble inside, wondering where to begin.

Even in this neighborhood where there is too much ugliness, I can find beauty and signs of hope. I can use my imagination to see a better place, one built from networks of relationships that transcend fear. I have picked out a house that I could live in with my family; it has large vacant lots on either side. I went back there to take pictures of it just today—the second of January. It's a striking house with a square cupola on the third floor with windows facing in every direction. It predates the era of suburban flight. The windows are big to let in the light, and the exterior woodwork is ornate and painted in Victorian hues. There is a young maple growing next to the house, something that blew in on the wind. The lot to the east has a sidewalk leading to where the front steps of another house once stood. I can see a crazy mixed-up vegetable and flower garden here and maybe a sour cherry tree, too.

Moving to this house and living here would change me, change my family. It would make our lives into part of story this landscape tells. I wonder how our decision would be narrated in the urban history. Would we be invaders? Could we be friends? Might I be a physician to this place? As a physician, would my intentions matter to the outcome? Could I make it a better place to live by choosing to live here with my family?

What drove me to medical school from my career in urban planning was the context of illness. I saw so much illness directly linked to how neighborhoods, communities, cities, and towns are developed. People live in neighborhoods like this and emerge from them to seek care, or they live in them in ill health because they can't afford to get it. If they could, their neighborhoods would not be pockmarked with vacant and burned houses.

We can drift and settle here, and root into place—and then by our very determination to live under a fearless sky begin to heal these places and ourselves. With each visit to this neighborhood, I become more comfortable. I recognize buildings. I have associations with places and people. My feelings have changed. My eyes see differently. I am not afraid. I am not the same. As I have small encounters with these places, as I venture into the stores and have conversations with the people who work here and live near here, this place becomes less of a stereotype of a bad neighborhood and more a particular place with a particular set of people, houses, and shops. It has become peculiar and distinct. It is not just a place full of stereotypical problems—the lead poisoning, STDs, AIDS, teen pregnancy, alcohol and drug abuse, homelessness, illegal immigrants, entrenched poverty, low-birth-weight babies.

Instead, it is the Ghanian shop owner who used to work in Albany landscaping for the state and the scrap metal collector with his upstairs tenant and the lifeguard studying to become a police officer. It is the beautiful old bones of houses and the vacant lots that grow weeds in the meantime, while whispering to passers-by that they could be more than a patch of green. They whisper to me, "Something more could grow here—much more. I was once something else. I can grow wild, unnoticed things for now, but I could be more. See me, know me, imagine me into something again, something fine."

First Words

Jennifer Richter

Child, you were light all at once.
You did not tunnel toward the bright
world waiting; from a small slit
like a crimp in the blinds, they pulled you
from me and held you to the sky,
held you crying, held you shining,
your fair skin lit from the inside,
your hair one huge fine red flame.
Luke, luminous, we chose the name
before we were sure of you
and since you came, our usual season
of rain has stayed away. Today,
sun strong at our backs, day of the year's
longest night, you sit on my lap,
wave your arm in the most deliberate
gesture I've seen, follow the spread
of your fingers across the floor
and just like that add shadows
to what you already know.
Already, you have a song-like voice
though it has taken four months
and this moment to coax my first words.
Strange, this turning from you to the page
so I wait until I hear the poem
whole in my head. Luke: the one
who found words for that one birth,
that famous star. In this season,
son, you live in holy mouths.
When you were born the doctors
held you up with arms raised,
and all our faces tilted to the place
blessings come from, and names,
and the first words, and light. Luke,
luminous, your hand in the air is a star;
on the floor our shadow is still one body.

Sleeping and Waking

Daniel Corrie

I am the next layer on those things
that have happened already.
—Andy Goldsworthy

My mother bragged that she would stab my father
some night in his sleep. Who was this Southern girl
who finally drank herself into my mother?

Before he entered guestroom sleep, my father
slid a magazine inside his shirt to shield
his heart from sudden steel and from my mother.

Arms tightening in drowsiness, my father
dodged a kitchen knife his dreams could feel.
His waking arms crisscrossed to block my mother.

To tame his dreaming arms, my father
cut tops and bottoms from Quaker oatmeal
cardboard tubes. Fighting off my mother,

he wore those sleeves. That way, my father
rode through the scenes of sleep with elbows held,
locked in the cereal cylinders my mother

emptied making breakfasts for my brother
and me, on mornings when the kitchen smelled
of bacon frying. In the bedroom, my father

buttoned his colonel's jacket, by its lapel
the Silver Star. Some other day, my mother
left. We seldom spoke of her to one another.

Wrong and right seemed dreams, each like the other.
Time bled my past, reddening like a future.
I would stitch each year, slow suture after suture.

Shelter by Night

Rokhsanna Sadeghi

With the flashlight peering over my shoulder, I pressed his head in one hand as I scraped the grit-and-blood-filled wound with the other. It was approximately ten p.m. on Wednesday night in Johannesburg's city-center. The arid, dark sky filled the silence that lingered in the streets. From the window of a passing car, the only visible life was the prostitutes scattered on street corners. But once I walked down the main streets and into the alleyways, I realized that the market that occupies this space during the day doesn't close down after dark.

I stepped out of the car and faced a city building illuminated by street lights in the black night. This was far from the well-furnished, newly renovated buildings that crowd cities in the U.S. Rather, this building was burned, all but the ground floor, and positioned between two four-story abandoned buildings. In Johannesburg, though, abandoned buildings are almost never truly abandoned. When I first looked at the door-less black hole I was to enter, I couldn't believe that life stirred within the smoke-scarred walls and crumbling cement.

With a flashlight, two bottles of multivitamins, two bottles of painkillers, two bottles of flu medicine, and most importantly, two bottles of rub-rub (an ointment that dulls muscle pain), I left behind the comfort of the warm, safe car and passed into a different world. Past the entrance, there were about fifteen people hunched around a fire in a small tin can. It consumed anything it was fed, scrap wood, cardboard, loose papers, and plastic. Just beyond the fire, I could barely make out a stretch of cardboard and cloth that separated and defined each person's home.

I turned off my flashlight and allowed my eyes to adjust to the darkness. I walked from the fire to the back of the building and counted about fifteen "rooms." Stealing glimpses into the rooms, candles illuminated babies on mats bundled tight against the crisp winter air, frail elderly people laid out on the beds, cloths and clothing slung on ropes, and magazines and dirty pots.

I made my rounds. Knocked on whatever I could find for a door and was invited in. I was greeted with broad smiles and teeth clenched with pain. I offered whatever I could. Often feeling helpless, I would retreat to the back of the sedan for a medical referral.

At the end of the night, as I was waiting beside the car, a young boy of about thirteen approached me, head slung, feet dragging. I asked how I could help him and he pointed to the left side of his head, just above his ear. I focused my flashlight to that area to see if I could tell what was bothering him. Glowing in my light was a two-inch wound, crusted with blood and dirt. The area has swollen larger than a golf ball.

"What happened?"

A slurred murmur replied, "I was hit in the head with a brick…when caught stealing."

Is this youthful, soft soul going to ripen into a tough, street-bound man? Grasping his head to clean the wound, my heart expanded to encompass my fears of the streets, of my vulnerability when walking in the crowded city-center market. All my emotion was focused on this child and tears filled my eyes to think of the life that he is so deserving of.

Pamela Ferris-Olson ~ *Nighttime Still Life*

Fall Morning

Lorraine Bruno Arsenault

October morning rises spare—
thin yellowed fingers,
loath to leave their cloudblanket,
slip a cool hand along
the back of a wide-eyed doe.
I stand at wood's edge
shadowed in the last of night,
eye-to-eye with the deer.
Alert to the heckle of a crow's caw,
she bends her head,
lifts her heels,
leaps away. And I?
I slip into the dark maze
of slick black tree trunks.
Tree bones crack against my legs,
leaf palms slide beneath my soles,
earthhollows beg at my feet.
I find her there again—
not her face—but her fear
when hasty thief September last
dropped her in the midnight forest,
stilled her voice,
deadened her limbs,
left her jeweled eyes
to peer through forest murk.
I fall by her side, offer warmth,
watch as a lone ray sifts through
tangled boughs, touches her heart,
gathers her light back to the sun.

Star Break

Anne Jacobson Ryan

Nurse on the graveyard shift
does the stats
hands out an occasional Ambien
avoids the polarity trap:
the argument on the floor
between Born Again and Liberal Muslim
smiles, says
"let's just do our jobs
come to my garden this summer
have tea
enjoy the roses
that we love as roses
and the lilies
that we love as lilies"

goes out with the smokers on break
to see the constellations
to take a star break.

Refrigerator

Sara Baker

You want me to keep
my feelings on ice.
You want me to be
a big white refrigerator,
all angles and quiet hinges.
And all those bloody,
messy parts—the old ghosts
and the fresh wounds—
you want packaged in tupperware:
orderly, neat.

I don't want to be a refrigerator.
I want to cook
my griefs, my fears, my sadness.
I want to take the lids off and sniff,
let the blood drain in the sink,
mix some fresh herb—lovage, maybe,
or hope,
into the pot full of sticky losses:
my absent mother
my angry brothers.
I want the kettle of my night terrors
to shriek
and fill the kitchen with steam.
And then, I want
to sit down and taste
the saltiness of regret
the bitterness of anger.
Then I will know who I am.
Then I will know I am alive.

The Story of My Life

Pamela L. Laskin

Charades: A Narrative in Two Voices

You walk into a circus. The screams are as loud as sirens. The performers are not following the script, though; they jump around like monkeys on the loose. The seven-foot giant, old and disheveled, wears a faded-blue terry robe, beneath which there is nothing but scarred, naked flesh. He is oblivious to the smells here—not hay, not elephant dung—but an odd mixture of excrement and urine. The giant moves, zombie-like, looking for an exit from the sights and smells. Old women jump up and down, only there's no trampoline, just the hard wooden floor, and when an eighty-year-old woman dressed in a flower-printed "schmata" falls down and bangs her head, she cries out, "Mama, mama." Instead, a nurse drags her down the floor, annoyed.

"Haven't I told you to cut it out, Sadie. I've told you too many times to stop playing like that."

Sadie's cries are reduced to whimpers.

In another corner, a young man starts to dance. The audience applauds, though Sadie, by this time, is screaming, "God is dead; God is dead." You think, perhaps he is.

In yet another ring is the woman you have come to visit. You have seen her performances numerous times in your forty-nine-year lifetime. She wears make-up like a clown. The red is smeared on her mouth and chin. You know the woman who always looks unkempt; she left you forty-five years ago to join the circus because she couldn't take care of you. Now she is screaming and flailing her arms randomly. She doesn't recognize you. Her act is wild; even a lion-tamer couldn't tame her, though he tries Haldol, and for a few fleeting moments you see the recollection of what she once was—a beautiful young bride your father had married in a moment of insanity. They call this place Coney Island Psychiatric Hospital. You have toured other circuses like this one. You've been forced to visit her. Your father has made you. You're mad at him for this manipulative coercion. Now she is more difficult to medicate. There are voices that somersault in her head. You drift off to the lullaby of ranting and raving.

* * *

"Let me in," I cry but not too loudly, for fear that the neighbors will hear. I am four years old and my fingers are frozen icicles. I have been playing outside in the snow for hours. The year is 1958; the place, Queens, New York; the houses face each other with boredom. Their flatness is a result of their lot in life—Garden Apartments. The neighbors are bored, too; consequently, they love to gossip. My home is a source of "good gossip." Screams always "raise the roof high."

Still, I like living here, on the first floor of a two-story apartment. I have dozens of friends in this development. They all know that the woman I live with ("my father's wife," I call her) is crazy.

"Let me in," I shriek, a little louder this time. She doesn't answer.

"I'm freezing." The dungeon of darkness has already settled outside. I am not allowed to stay out when it's dark; I have promised Father. She won't let me in, and I refuse to ask for help from the neighbors.

I huddle in the corner of the vestibule like a big rubber ball, one that lions use to roll around on. I cry silently to myself.

Hours later, Father arrives home; my tears are frozen on my face, and I have peed in my pants. He pushes the door open, races in, throws her on the floor and starts screaming, "You bitch; you bitch." Over and over he screams while she lies there on the floor, helpless and panting. There is no place left to hide. The neighbors know everything.

* * *

You are back here, again. It's a new place for her, for you. It's called Creedmore State. You have watched them take her away, surprised by the magic—no arms. The white harness has made her arms disappear. So many people in this place are strapped to their beds. They howl like animals in heat; they want out of the zoo. And she wants to feel her hands. It's just a trick. Later you will see her arms fly wildly as if they are caught in an air pocket. You want to be one of two things—maybe an aerialist. Then you imagine you are a tightrope walker, and you must not fall, ever. Your father is crying, but you don't help him; you are too busy keeping the balance. Why did your father bring you here? There's music of screaming voices in the background. She tells you she loves roses—pink and yellow. You are five years old and can't buy her any since you don't even get an allowance.

* * *

"Do you know this woman?"

We are in Gimbel's department store, and the security guard has just made a house arrest. He has her hand-cuffed. She has tried to steal a pink ballroom gown she insists was hers in another lifetime. There are assorted bright shades of department store lipstick in her bag, too.

"No." I stand outside the dressing room, six years old, scrawny, well trained as a contortionist. I have already learned the skills to get me out of any situation.

"Isn't she your mother?"

"No." I gaze at the ground. "If she were, wouldn't she act like she knows me?" I ask him, nonchalantly.

He scratches his beard.

"I need to call my father," I tell him.

I always need to call my father who will rescue me like Prince Charming on his white horse. If he were a serious rescuer, though, he'd be Houdini and get rid of her once and for all.

* * *

This time you are an aerialist. The music is loud, and it makes you certain you can fly. You know the drugged-out inhabitants all too well; their poses show crippled excitement. Their costumes are ripped and tattered. She tells you, her face contorted but blank, "The doctor is in love with me. He's young and cute. He's not the only one, though. One of the female nurses loves me too." Then she continues, "I need more jewelry, if you can buy me some."

Behind her are other adults, their faces elastic with joy. You smile; your act is worse than hers.

* * *

"According to the divorce agreement, you have to see her every other week." My father is insistent.

"Can't I get divorced from her?"

My father walks away. He's used to this argument. He doesn't understand. None of my friends in our new neighborhood know about her. Here in Flushing with a stepmother and my father, everything is anonymous. My friends believe my stepmother is my mother. What if my charade is unearthed while walking the streets with this woman? I ask to meet her at an ice skating rink in Brooklyn, far enough away so no one will know me. It's in Prospect Park where the skeleton arms of the trees reach for the sky.

"The sky is the limit," she often says since she adores clichés. Father promises to pick me up in a few hours. As soon as I arrive, she is there, smiling, jubilant to see me. She shoves a package into my hands. I open it—a black velvet skater's skirt lined with red silk.

"Oh my God! I've wanted this for ages." I look around suspiciously, then kiss her quickly on the cheek.

"I know," she says, the arc of triumphant pleasure crowning her face.

"How did you know?"

"It's all you ever talk about." She is beaming.

* * *

You are fifteen, and you hate everything. You hate the fact that your father has died, leaving you alone with your stepmother. It could have been worse. You could have been left alone with her.

When you walk in, all eyes turn on you like seething bullets. You enter through a gated, padlocked door that the doctor has opened. A few people race to the gate like animals ready to leave their cages, but they can't. Why did your father have to die when you were only fourteen years old? You are ready for the kill.

"Oh my darling, oh my darling, oh my darling Clementine," she sings, so happy to see you.

"I am not Clementine."

"I know that," she says, with a silly grin on her face. "You are my Fagye."

"I'm not that, either."

"Oh yes you are," she announces self-assuredly.

"What is that—a Fagye?" You want to rip apart that smiling clown face of hers.

"It means bird of paradise. It's your Jewish name."

"Oh."

"How's your father, by the way?"

"He's dead."

"Oh!"

In the side ring, a singer entertains. He belts out Frank Sinatra, and the ladies jump up and down. When they start singing and asking for autographs, the nurses are poised with their spears of medication. You wish you could get medicated too and think of jumping out the window in a wild trapeze act. Maybe you are crazy too. Perhaps it's just that you are fifteen.

* * *

The older I get, the less frequently I see her. The "visitation rights" according to the divorce seem obsolete. Her family stops calling me. I never forgave her sister when I heard how vehemently she had argued for "joint custody," as if this woman could have raised me.

When I am in my twenties, she moves into a small studio in Coney Island. From her window, I can see the remains of the dying Cyclone. She has a woman who stays with her, and she and the woman sit on lawn chairs in the summer, staring mutely at the sidewalks. She told me, once, there were alien visitors in the cracks of the sidewalks, so she avoids them when she can.

I avoid her. Sometimes I visit and stay for an hour or so; we have nothing to say. She asks about my father, and I remind her that he's dead.

I don't invite her to my wedding, to my son's bris, to any important occasions. Sometimes when I am there, she goes on a screaming rampage—a non-stop twenty-minute vocalization. Maybe it's her rage. During these episodes, she is sometimes taken away to another "place."

I rarely bring my children to see her since they find her scary. They know her as "Granny" and can't quite figure out her connection to me. It's better this way.

*   *   *

You return. You are almost fifty; your fiftieth birthday is only months away. Your son is in college and your daughter is in high school. The show is over. You have finally come to realize that these are not performers; they are the real thing. The smell of urine bombards your nostrils like an evil villain. The walls have grown uglier, dirtier, and chips crumble off the ceiling like gaping wounds, exposing holes that fester. She is almost eighty years old. You know that she will die here, they all will die here, because this is no longer a psychiatric hospital but a nursing home.

The inhabitants are not like animals in their cages; the padlocked doors are gone. The people amble slowly with their walkers or in their wheelchairs. Everyone is old and tired, so they choose to stay inside, even in the summer, staring at the television, their saviors. Besides, permission must be granted to sit on a bench outside, and most of them have lost their voice and their desire. They sit inside and wait. Many of them have no visitors, not ever.

You wish you could leave this woman, but you wear your pain like a tattoo. You can feel sorry for her, though, and stop feeling sorry for yourself. You have the privilege to walk out the door and smell the sunshine and flowers of spring. She is here forever—trapped in her body, stuck in a room with screams and smells and zombies, a room you visit and leave.

You know this woman well; she is your mother. The pretense is over. She would give anything to be a part of your family, a role you've taken away from her. Lately, though, you have been visiting her more.

"You have been seeing your mom a lot," says your husband.

"I know."

"Why?"

"I feel sorry for her. Besides, I'm not so angry anymore. She has had no choice. She really loves me."

And when you walk into her room, her whole face lights up.

"Will you visit me again—soon? And perhaps bring the children."

You promise to come next week with the children, her grandchildren, and bring pink and yellow roses.

Yolanda Tooley ~ *Still Life with Zebra*

Ellen Giraud ~ *Swallow Your Pride*

Ellen Giraud ~ *The Egg*

Locked Ward

Valerie Wohlfeld

Two o'clock: all the daughters
waited for their mother's visit.
I waited for my mother in her brocade of rose water.
That every rose weds the bee, I found exquisite.

Two o'clock: the doors unlocked to let the mothers in.
One girl, out of her scars, said sibylline:
not bruise but blood was rising under skin.
Each of us were as Ming porcelain

on a ship of treasures going down to sea.
In four weeks the bee rips through its set of wings.
We would inherit our mother's roses on her china cup of tea.
Like Odysseus we couldn't hear the sirens sing.

One girl said bruise was only veins rising under skin.
Two o'clock: the doors unlocked to let the mothers in.

Kasai Procedure: A Snapshot

Maureen Picard Robins

No shrub of the field was yet in the earth. [Gen 2:5]
Rabbi Simeon went on to say the allusion is to the magnificent trees which grew later, but as yet were minute.
—The Zohar

We don't know what he will see once he opens the baby;
we are cowards shivering before God's white glare
seeking healing, transformation from broken to whole,
melting skin, soldered seams of stained strained hearts
and all the love that Dr. Altman can give us.

We surrender her into the arms of the anesthesiologist
who throws a warmed yellow blanket over her,
a chick's color, flattened feather fuzz,
the yolk's nourishing sack a ghostlike reminder
of where she was so safe not long ago.
Dr. Altman says, *We'll do our best.*

We wait upstairs seated at the edge of the bed
staring out a window, seeing myself, as if I am
my own guardian angel, dangling from steel rafters
in the sanitary sanctuary.

A rabbi stops in to chat, sits in a vinyl chair that gasps.
Don't want to talk. Don't need a rabbi. Have direct access.
Watching heaven's clouds flecked with baby teeth
and fractured souls waiting for human homes.
Clouds roll by; beds on wheels for resting messengers,
metal stretchers for exhausted angels awaiting their next assignment;
some supine belted in but with just enough strength left
to lift a head and peek in

when Dr. Altman sprints in and sits lightly:
It was worse than we thought.
He untwisted her intestines and slit microscopic incisions

to vent the flesh that should have openings, to be soft, porous,
so bile could tremble down the liver's pitted walls, to recreate
the biliary tree within her, within us, because now we know
what it is like to be expelled from Paradise.

Kasai Procedure: A Thought Shot

> *The surgeon removes the damaged ducts outside the liver and replaces them with a piece of the baby's own intestine. This new duct allows bile to pass from the liver to the intestine. . . . With an experienced surgeon the kasai procedure is successful in sixty to eighty percent of the patients.*
>
> —*Children's Hospital of Cincinnati's website explaining kasai procedure*

What was Dr. Altman thinking on his way to the room where I was waiting? My feet swing beneath the metal edge of the bed. There was only the sound of his soft-soled shoes, thoughts so loud I thought I heard him wondering what words to tell me, what words to use that would give me hope, that wouldn't promise false hope, and I wondered whether or not he was thanking God or hating him and why he takes on only the most difficult of cases the babies who will be so loved but won't live. What does Dr. Altman think when that phone rings and there's another of God's mistakes, another innocent with a liver without a duct, an incomplete tree, *Not another one*, then says, *Come in,* as though he will still your shaking shoulders and argue your side before God with quick, efficient movements of the hand, the twirling fire between his fingers. So neat. And after you've adjusted to this news and adjusted your thinking about paradise as you knew it, he'll give you guidelines on how to recreate it and it will be lined with your insides and everybody knows nothing will ever be the same.

Failed Kasai: The baby needs a liver to live

The authors analyzed risks for failure in 266 patients treated from 1972-1996. . . .
Failure was defined as death or transplant.
—*Altman, R. Peter, M.D., Flanigan, Laura, R.N.* Annals of Surgery *226(3): 348-355*

No matter
fluorescent incandescent
dimmed wattage high voltage
yellow is yellow is yellow
under any kind of light
at any time of night
when ghosts shadow sleep
and I wait to wake
to feed her
sweet potatoes on a nipple
hiding a dusting of Actigall
a bitter powder for her liver

to lay her on a changing table
looking for green
in what she excretes
the broken yolk in the whites
of her eyeballs
the amber syrup
of worn blood cells
staining the seventh layer
of skin
barely draining
from the tissue
closest to her soul

I must use my eyes
as never before
I look at her
as Dr. Altman examines
and thinks out loud
a month post Kasai

to see if she smiles
has grown at all
and the numbers
from the blood test
we don't need
because her color
tells it all

Dr. Altman will not say
"failed Kasai"
or communicate
failure with his eyes
rather
he did all he can
and now
we don't know
if she will live
but we won't give up

he'll phone
Dr. Dunn
and list her for
transplant.

That night after midnight
under the shower of fluorescent light
I wash dishes
in the kitchen sink.
Sponge and water
chant meditations
and form snapshots
in my head of
of the baby playing in spring grass.

She stirs and wakes.
I cradle her in my arms
and lay her on the changing table
massage her jaundiced skin
with a soothing balm
to draw off the itch.
Each fingertip transmits
my wishes and dreams.

36 Hours Before the Transmigration of Souls

For love is strong as death, violent, as is the separation of the spirit from the body and only with great rending is its separation performed.
—The Zohar

Marooned in a hospital room,
washed up at the side of her bed,
grief-weighted. Behind me
nurses bend over my baby
as if tying her to a life raft
of her mattress,
as if by inserting needles
in each rubbery arm and ankle
they will anchor her
before she falls back
into the primordial ocean.

God has withdrawn
into his innermost self.

Dr. Dunn enters and tells us
he will transplant the baby
not at eight a.m. but later,
that we must wait for a surgeon
to helicopter in from Wisconsin
to take the heart
from the brain-dead baby
on another floor.
He suggests rest.

I will not wander
in a white dream
where I can't hear her breathe
or leave her before the hour.
I will be the *shomer,* the watcher,
of the intermingling souls,
the rotating helixes afloat,

waiting for an unseen moment
to flee.

When the nurses depart
I lie with my daughter. My heart chants
through chest wall and cheek bone
as I transfuse every last drop of myself.
Dr. Dunn summons us at noon.
Before the double doors of the OR
I give her a kiss.
The shadow of my lips imprints
on the porous cushion of her skin.
Now she will get a liver,
a maroon-colored sponge
cut from the donor baby
and she will absorb him
and who we are
and all we live for
the bonds of blood
all my heavy love.

Midnight Angel

Mark J. Sicherman

Sherman began his third sleepless night in the ICU with a short, silent prayer to anyone who might be listening and perhaps be able to do something. *Please don't let me die in the night. If I have to die, which, you should understand, is not something I want, please let it be in the daytime, surrounded by my loved ones.*

He refused the sleeping pill offered by the evening charge nurse before she went off duty at eleven. When she asked why, he just shrugged. She didn't seem like the kind of person who would understand his need to remain vigilant.

A few minutes later, Julie the night nurse made her rounds. Sherman realized that she was very pretty. He'd been too sick to notice before tonight. Still, she weighed at least 220. He supposed that everyone who saw her said to themselves, why would such a beautiful girl let herself go like that. Sherman knew she must have her reasons. Julie stood at the foot of the bed, put her hand on his left foot and squeezed gently. She looked right at him, held his gaze without smiling and asked, "Are you feeling any better tonight, doctor?"

Sherman could have cried with gratitude. He couldn't know, of course, if she really cared, but if she didn't, it didn't matter. It was a perfect imitation of caring, and it worked. The others, all the others, doctors, nurses, aides, lab techs breezed in with a fake smile and a new-waitress voice, looking at the chart instead of him, and asked, brightly, "How are *we* doing?" It made him want to scream.

He managed a smile. "I am feeling a little better tonight. Thanks, Julie. And I'd rather you call me Sherman." He hesitated, then revealed more than he intended. "But to tell you the truth, I'm really scared."

Julie said nothing. She pulled a chair closer to the bed and sat on the edge of it, her hands open to him, as if waiting for more.

Sherman fought the tears welling up in his eyes. He cleared his throat several times. "You know that guy, what's his name, the *hospitalist*?"

She must have detected the bitterness. "Resnick. You don't like him either, huh?"

Sherman grinned and nodded. "Permission to speak freely?"

Julie rolled her eyes. "Hey listen, Sherman, you can say anything you want." She laughed. "Especially about Resnick."

Sherman laid his head back on the pillow and sighed. "Asshole. Goddam fucking incredibly insensitive asshole! He came in earlier today, when my son and daughter-in-law were visiting. He was frowning at my chart like he didn't know who I was, and he kept flipping back and forth to the lab reports. 'Little problemo here,' he says, still with his nose in the chart and one foot out the door."

Sherman sat up straight in bed and did his best to imitate Resnick's nasal fast-talk.

"'White count was down a little on admission—4200, which we attributed to septic shock. The next morning she dropped to 3800 and this a.m., powie, 2600. Not a good sign. We may have to ship you to University if she continues to drop.' And then he says. I couldn't believe it. He says, 'Just hang in there, chief. Try to relax. We'll see which way she's going in the morning.'"

"Oh, God, Sherman, that's awful," said Julie. "He really said try to relax?"

Sherman pounded his fist, the one without the IV, into the bed. "I could not believe it. I fucking could not believe it. I just went numb all over—you know, like paralyzed with fear. But I had to make light of it for my kids. I told them it was probably nothing to worry about, and I tried to make small talk. But goddamit, I can't get it out of my mind. I keep thinking 2600 and dropping. My God. Acute agranulocytosis. People die from that. No wonder they want to ship me out. Don't die in my hospital." Sherman, his anger spent, lay back on the pillow and stared at the overhead fluorescence.

"After the kids left, I asked the charge nurse to page Resnick, to get him back here so I could ask him, like, what's causing this, and what can we do about it, and why the hell wait until tomorrow for another white count. But she wouldn't. He's way too busy for that, she told me."

Sherman glanced over at Julie. Her face was red, very red, and her lower lip was trembling. She rose from the chair slowly. At first he thought it was her weight, holding her back. Then he realized that she was struggling with something far heavier than her bulk. She paused by the bedside and squeezed his free hand.

"I'll be right back," she said, her voice husky.

While he was waiting for Julie's return, Sherman's body began trembling, first his legs, then a shaking in his chest. He kept his jaw clamped shut. To open it, he knew, would be to risk sobbing like a child.

Julie re-appeared at his bedside. Her color had returned to normal. "I called the lab tech at home and told him that Resnick had ordered a stat white count on you. He'll be here in about thirty minutes to draw the blood, then another fifteen for the results. I also asked Melanie to cover my other patients for the next hour."

Julie sat again in the side chair. "We're going to see this through together," she said. She didn't exactly smile, at least not with her mouth, but her eyes were bright.

Sherman let go of a long, ragged breath. His body relaxed. "Thank you," he whispered, and for a few seconds he must have dozed because when he awoke, with a start, his mouth was cottony. He sat up and looked at her.

"Julie. My God! I just realized. You could get in big trouble for this. I mean you don't have a written or verbal order from Resnick. What if he finds out?"

"I had to do it," she said. "I'm sick of his arrogance. I've never done anything like this before. I suppose it has something to do with this being my last night."

"Last night?"

She sighed. "I don't know if you want to hear all this," she said.

"Every word," he said. "Please."

Julie stood up. "Look at me," she said, doing a little pirouette in her size eighteen nurse's uniform, holding the hem of her jacket between thumb and forefinger, the rest of her fingers splayed delicately outward like the ribs of a fan. She began pacing as she talked, slowly at first, then with some urgency. From time to time she stopped and faced Sherman squarely, hands on hips, and spoke fiercely, but softly, like a mother trying not to wake the baby.

Sherman listened as if his life depended on it. He knew how to do this, to make everything else disappear from his world except the person across from him, hearing the words, observing shifts in color and tone, knowing what was going on inside her as surely as if it were happening in his own body.

She was getting out of town. She had taken a job as nursing supervisor in a small hospital in Vermont. A place where no one knew her and where she could make a fresh start. Maybe there she could lose weight for real. Maybe then she could meet a guy. She needed to be far from dad, who had loved her too much. And from mom who had let it happen. And from her little brothers who made fun of her from the time she was fifteen and the pounds started piling up into layers of protection. And from her stupid, useless therapist who kept telling her if she could only see how beautiful she was she wouldn't do this to herself. And from her friends who downloaded new diets for her almost daily. And from the other nurses who took advantage of the fact that she had no life and got her to work nights and weekends for them.

The lab tech came and drew the blood. A few minutes later Julie went out to the nurses' station to await the faxed results. When she left, Sherman felt the fear creep back into his belly, freezing him from the inside out. He tried to concentrate on Julie's plight instead of his own, but it was useless. He had to admit he'd rather be fat than dead. He kept his eyes fixed on the doorframe, waiting for Julie to appear.

Suddenly she was standing in the doorway, as if she had dropped from the sky. She was holding a sheet of paper in both hands, staring at it. Her mouth was open. She looked like a choirgirl about to sing a hymn. Gradually her face broke into a smile. It was the biggest, most beautiful, most welcome smile Sherman had ever seen. She floated toward the bed, her eyes shining. She held the report out to him.

"5200," she said, breathlessly.

"5200!" Sherman shouted. "5200!"

He opened his arms to her, not heeding the IV in his left wrist. They hugged, awkwardly, Julie leaning over the bed, Sherman straining to get his arms around her. She kissed his cheek. He cried a little. Then laughed and cried some more.

"You are an angel," he said. "No, more than that. I'm recommending you for sainthood. How can I ever thank you?"

"Wish me well in Vermont," she said.

"With all my heart," he said.

When Julie left the room, Sherman adjusted his pillow and stretched out on the bed. He knew sleep would come now. Before it did, his mind raced to find a way to express the gratitude he felt in his chest. Julie had saved his life. He was sure of it. If it hadn't been for her, the white count would have gone the other way. It was not something he could tell anyone, but he knew it was true. He would buy Julie a Porsche. No, better a Mercedes. He would save her life: He would move to Vermont, see her every day, help her to lose weight, stay there until she was happily married. Perhaps he would be the one to give her away.

In the morning, when he awoke, she was gone. He smiled.

"Be well and happy, Julie," he whispered into the room.

Susannah Loiselle ~ *Window at St. Peter's Barn*

Job's Neck

Alexander Douglas Grant

I met a girl in NYC who I got on with and who invited me up to Martha's Vineyard, an island where her family owned property and spent the summer. I had just bought the only new car I have ever owned, a 1976 fjord blue 2002 BMW, with sunroof, and with her at the wheel we made our way along the Cape to the ferry. We stopped along the way, and I had my first real New England meal since I traveled there with my family in the mid-fifties. The coast hadn't changed much, which was nice. There were still lots of grey shacks by the water and the curious obsession with lobsters was unchanged.

In passing, I remember telling her that my roommate Mark and I had an agreement to kidnap the other if either of us contemplated marriage. Her face was expressionless when I said it. She had just finished lighting a cigarette with the car lighter. I think something changed then. Later, I thought she had accepted it as a challenge, and I felt flattered by her sly maneuvers to keep Mark at a distance. Of course it wasn't just him. She was culling the herd (as a serious girl should). Eventually, other old friends dropped away.

In a remarkably short time, we had a little house on the Katama Road and our visit had become "a summer." More hers than mine. I still worked weekdays in New York. That meant weekend flights on Air New England for me. The house was filled during the week with friends from the city who made room for me, sometimes reluctantly, when I arrived Friday night. The car was left there for her to use.

Her family was charming and welcomed me into their usual Vineyard summer. They were unpretentious and at ease on their own ground. And their grounds were very special. They had the largest private beach on the island, and even on the Fourth of July you could look up and down its length and not see another soul.

On one of those weekends, we went to our favorite spot, Job's Neck. This was the area between Job's and the next pond. These brackish ponds lay behind the ocean dunes, and their warm, still waters were a silken counterpoint to the rough surf of the ocean. Job's Pond was the prettiest of the lakes behind the dunes. If you stood on the shore and looked over the grasses into the bordering woods, you saw America as the Pilgrims did when their boat first bumped the rock.

We had a picnic one day, some wine and other things. The young people in her family and a good friend of mine, who had spent the week, were all there.

Having not shared the weekdays with them, it took a bit of time for the city to wear off. It was almost like being a tourist among natives, but it always passed after awhile. Not immediately part of the cooking, games, or banter, I headed off alone for a quick swim in the ocean. It was a perfect day. High blue sky, glaring sun, and a steady breeze off the sea.

I went in about twenty yards from the group, not right in front of them. I guess I still felt a little left out and put some distance between us. I walked to about chest depth, hopping over the active surf and swam further down the beach. In the course of a few seconds I found myself twice as far from shore as I should have been.

I tried to swim back to the beach. I just kept drifting toward Spain. I waved and shouted for help. I saw them, but they didn't see me. Instantly desperate, I dove to the bottom without thinking. It was the nearest land. The beach had dropped off below me, and it was a long way down to the bottom. I grabbed at the sand with my hands and for a few seconds dragged myself toward the beach. When the next wave came I rode it to the surface, gasped some air and dove back down. I repeated this like a machine. As long as I went under immediately after breathing, I could hold my own and even (I imagined) make headway.

I lost track of time before I got to the sharp slope where the beach falls off. I was already tired. The pull of the undertow increased in the shallower water of the slope. The sand was different. It was filled with little rocks and littler pieces of shell churning in an emulsion of half floating sand. As I clawed toward land, the debris at the bottom, dragged back by the waves, scoured my arms and face. My body would lift and flail in the water like a branch in a stiff wind.

I kept crawling. When I felt the wave come, I would pull my knees to my chest and dive up through the water toward the air, breathe, and dive down again before I could be dragged too far back.

When I got to a point where the water was no longer over my head, I still had to keep diving to the bottom. The pull of the rip tide was too strong, and upright I was in danger of being dragged backwards. I don't think I could have withstood the setback of losing ground. By this time I was spiritually invested in the incremental rescue I was performing on myself. Though fatigued, the shorter distance to the surface acted like a tonic, and I continued.

At the end, I knew I was safe when I could just stand, fall forward with the waves' motion and still make progress. Soon, I was crawling, with my head above the water. Even breathing at will, I couldn't crawl when the waves pulled out. I had to wait for the incoming wave to make my bit of progress. My muscles were cramped, my eyes fixed on the sand and the water, foaming and hissing beneath my eyes. I hadn't looked at the shore since I began diving and didn't now. When there were only inches of water around me, I struggled to stand. I shakily managed a sagging upright position our remote ancestors would have recognized.

Even in a few inches of water, I still couldn't walk forward in the receding waves. The water dragged at my ankles and held me to the spot as securely as concrete. When the drag stopped and the waters came in, I could stagger forward a little. I had become part of the surf.

When there was nothing beneath my feet but damp sand, the world seeped back into view. Things seemed so far off. The sun was still out. White clouds still sketched wispy patterns on a high blue sky. The forest around Job's Neck looked green, inviting, and even more virginal. But the distances were stupefying. I found I couldn't walk. I couldn't even speak. I had heard of people being drained of strength. It was no longer a figure of speech to me. Muscles I hadn't used were limp. Those I had used were loose rubber bands of pain.

I stood without moving with my eyes closed, warm sun and airy currents over my skin, the smell of salt hay drifting from over the dunes, but the sound of the sea at my back had my soul in thrall. The lapping sound wasn't pleasant to me any more. I didn't feel the same way about the beauties of the Neck either just then, or the whole idyllic island I had come to love. At the edge of all that beauty, right where you stopped looking, was horror. The underside of those perfect beaches could kill. In literature, the parted veil is usually represented as a positive opportunity for the soul. I'm doubtful of that.

My strength came back surprisingly fast. It was a warm glow through my body. Its slow spread was welcome and miraculous. I was able to shuffle back to the others. I felt like a ghost at a party. They hadn't noticed anything. I had experienced an alien abduction right in front of them, and they hadn't noticed. I was inwardly a little angry at them. I wanted some company right then, and I didn't get it. There were some perfunctory expressions of concern when I mentioned my near-death experience, but I let it slide into a joke. It seemed that almost drowning on the Vineyard was like falling off your horse in hunt country, something to be passed over lightly. And I didn't press it.

I had believed there was a reservoir of care and affection for me on the island. It seemed to be true. Not that I needed it until my swim. But standing there, I felt the wrongness of it all. I knew that if she had been in the water, or anyone, I would have glanced over at them. It would have been ironic if they had seen me wave and had waved back not realizing my predicament. But I was sure they hadn't looked at me once. I put it out of my mind. I liked being back on the surface. I drew no conclusions. (The obvious has always eluded me.) I should have known though, about the undertow, about them and about her. I was a ghost there before I went in the water.

Shade

Beverly Boyd

> *"Suspicious finding . . . a partially ill-defined nodule in the 11 o'clock position. . . ."*
> —*Radiologist's diagnosis*

You'd think a gnomon on a sundial
that's never seen the sun had left
a wedge of red on an axis marking time:

thirty-three days of clicking light,
twenty-five with waves, eight of beta
particles, suffuse a three-inch slice

of irradiated flesh. An immodest blush
casts a spell between ten and twelve,
or in a mirror from twelve to two,

but looking down, I see red ochre
stretched between four and six.
How should I read this clock? two hours

or ten minutes only, all tolled, gained
or lost? From any angle it radiates
awareness, a wariness of time:

shadows emanating from light will fade,
or so I have been told.

Anybody Listening?

Robin Nagowski

I pour myself another cup of coffee, wishing it were seven and I could go home.
The coffee maker sizzles and burns the bottom of the pot as I slide it back
I stand there stealing a few more minutes, letting the sound soothe me
I try not to think about the last patient I saw
He didn't speak English, the third today
It takes so much energy to understand them while the time clicks forcing me forward
Reminding me that there's never enough.
What's the point?
I walk back to the nurses' station
My coffee sloshes in the Styrofoam cup, I don't even try to stop the spilling
As I walk past the patients I see a familiar face
Though it's certainly not familiar to him anymore
I know I will be seeing him next and I prepare for battle
I take him to the last room in the hall; the isolation might support intimacy and trust
I need him to trust me
You need to let me help you, I tell him. Stay here so we can help you
I stare at his jaw, almost disgusted, I can't imagine why he waited so long?
Why didn't you listen last time?
I know before he stutters that he isn't going to stay
They never do
They come to me for help then don't let me
I hand back his loose papers and soiled vanilla envelope knowing that the belongings
he offered will not help me convince him to stay
I ask him to come back tomorrow for treatment to begin, then I turn away
He won't return, he's done this before
I take another coffee in defeat and the bitter taste warms me
I close my eyes, count to ten, then walk back through dingy white hallways, past
patients lined up in anticipation, into section B.
I take the next patient

* * *

I don't know why I chose to come here today. To delay further I smoke a cigarette.
Maybe this will be my last
I smoke another

Inside, I need something to do with my hands; it would help pass the time.
Eternity is not the word I would choose but when my name is called I long for it. I
know there is something wrong and has been.
I can't look at myself in the mirror.
They talk to me, ask some questions then point me toward another piece of the maze.
Again I wait.
Time clicks, I fidget. Not out of worry or fear, but out of need.
I hear my name. He takes me to a room, far away in the shadows of the hall—is it
easier to look at me here? He talks, I think he is trying to help but I can't stay here.
No one would be able to take care of Mac, I tell him.
I show him a picture. I think he saw it, he must have.
I can't stay here I don't know what you want to do but I have to go home to Mac.
I need him
I go outside again, to breathe fresher air.
I light up and the taste warms me.
I reach for my jaw, habit, and remember what it used to feel like,
even if I stay here I doubt it would ever be the same.
I told that nice man I would return tomorrow for more tests, I think that's what he
wanted.
I know he doesn't expect to see me I've done this to him before, and others
But I can still breathe
I have Mac
I can't lose him because of this, what's the point?
I walk east along Bailey. Three more blocks, twenty more minutes if the bus is on
time, then I'm home.
Just me and Mac.

Lois Dorschel ~ *Winter Dam*

The Birth of Venus

Mehr-Afarin Hosseini
Dearing Writing Award, Honorable Mention
Student Division

And suddenly, it called my name,
And I became the bride of Acadias. . . .
—from Forough Farrokhzad, Let Us Believe in the Beginning of the Cold Season

The day after, as she opened her eyes, she first felt the heaviness of the blanket on her chest and then the sweat that covered her body. Rays of light had pierced through the blinds and disturbed her early morning sleep. As she opened her eyes, an anxious feeling swirled within her body and brought to her mind the deafening silence of those hot Sunday afternoons when Grandma, covered in her praying veil, took a nap on a sunny spot on the rug, and she worried as she was whispering to her doll, that she would wake Grandma up and make her grumpy. . . . She closed her eyes again, still feeling the heaviness of the blanket. Grandma had sewn that blanket many years ago, and if Ma had not taken it out again a fortnight before—on her eighteenth birthday—she would have left it to rot at the bottom of her closet for the rest of her life, as she had done since she was thirteen.

She could hear the dishes clatter in the kitchen. Someone was impatiently scrubbing a pan and a voice argued with itself in a whisper. Her dad banged the door and left. The burbling of water in a bowl and again an indistinct whisper. Tea, how much she wished for tea! Her mouth tasted bitter. Uneasily, she swallowed and with one hand grabbed and pulled the blanket on top of her head. On the blanket, little *khorshid khanooms*[1] were sewn in between the white and yellow squares: with their unibrows, almond eyes and innocent smiles that made their round faces, lined in small orange scarves, even rounder. Underneath the Qajar[2] miniatures, however, was only darkness. She wiped the sweat from her forehead and opened her eyes in the dark.

With last night, it had been exactly fourteen nights. Last night, like the nights before, she had heard the woman's voice in her head. Frightened, she had sat up on her bed and in the darkness of the window in between the blind strips had seen, for a slight moment, the faint ghost of the woman. Every night, she had

[1] Iranian Qajar miniatures that depict a prototypical Persian female face
[2] The Qajar dynasty was the ruling family of Persia from 1781 to 1925.

groped her way to every corner of the house looking for her, only to find not a soul but herself by the living room window, staring out at the black shadows of the mountains that surrounded Tehran. At night she felt the city was even more closed in by the smog that descended like a blanket. Every time, she had returned to bed with a suffocating cough and had squirmed restlessly on her pillow until morning. Last night too, like the other nights, she had gotten up. She had waited in the corridor for her eyes to adapt but froze when she reached the living room. By the window, the moonlight made apparent the curvy edge of a body. At first she could only distinguish the curve of her spine, then arms drawn around her chest and bent knees that seemed attached to the wall, indistinguishable from the ground in the darkness. The woman's face was hidden behind long black hair. When she called, the woman turned, and then she saw them with her own eyes, the moonlight lining the circle of her large breasts and the two red, ripe apples that were suspended within her loins, right under her navel. She saw them both through the transparent skin, with her very own eyes. . . .

At first, she had decided to run away. She had rushed back to her bedroom, her white nightgown twisting around her bare ankles. But as soon as she had reached the door, without any hesitation she had turned around and had run all the way back to the living room but had not seen the woman by the window anymore. She had put her forehead on the cold window, gaining her breath. A strange feeling crawled in her body like a snake. Cautiously touching her waist, she did not know why she had felt so anxious. . . .

* * *

Distressed, she ripped the blanket away from her head. She could hear her heart, beating. She kicked the blanket away and sat up, feeling her sweaty stomach.

Grandma was snoring under her flowery praying veil. Her huge rear that moved up and down with every breath hid her face. She was sitting at the corner of the rug, with a bowl of plums that Grandma had soaked well in water since morning, and she did not dare to move a finger lest she would wake Grandma up and make her grumpy. She crammed a fistful of wet plums in her mouth and the black shadows of her eyes roamed about the bright room in wonder.

* * *

She could hear Ma grumbling from the kitchen, calling and announcing to her that it was noon already and then to herself: *discipline has no meaning in this house anymore!* She pressed her palms on the bed and dragged herself to the edge. The nightgown crawled up to her middle. She hesitated, slipped back, and with both hands grabbed the blanket and pulled it up to her chest. She sat there for a while, with her gaze mindlessly fixed on the framed Persian cashmere on the wall. After a while, she lay down again and pulled the blanket all the way up to her chin. Cautiously she moved her hand under the nightgown and touched her waist. She pressed, higher, lower, underbelly. As her hand touched the thin hair, she withdrew it, curling it up under her breast. It was then that she remembered him. First his hands that yesterday in the secrecy of the stairways had circled around her, and then his lips that had stung her neck and the same good feeling. . . .But her eyes had stared at the white wall past his shoulder and the crack that had crawled up the wall like a snake. And her hands had involuntarily thrust away his hands that had glided their way up to her breasts, and now she could see his questioning eyes in front of hers again. His beautiful eyes, almond, almond eyes and the tasty bitterness of his mouth. But they were not kids anymore, they were not kids. . . .She pulled the blanket up to her mouth and bit it.

*   *   *

As the peddler peddled through the valley with his worn-out four-wheeler and sang with a cracked voice his *"salt for bread,"*[3] Grandma jerked under her veil and woke up. The sunlight bothered her eyes, and she held up the veil in frond of her face. She had stayed still with cheeks full of plums. Grandma turned to her.

"Little, little imp, with all the noise she makes, doesn't spare her old granny a little nap," Grandma said.

"It was the peddler," she tried to reply with a full mouth, but Grandma did not hear. She just pulled herself off the ground and wrapped up the veil and threw it to the corner of the room. Then as she rearranged the little combs in her dyed thinning hair, she came towards her, her heavy body tottering from side to side, and ripped the bowl away from her hands.

"Your tummy will get sick from all the plums you're eating. I better go make some sugar tea for you," she said. Then she walked away towards the kitchen, and left her motionless in the room with a lump in her throat.

*   *   *

She could hear Ma's flip-flops on the mosaics. She thought to herself that if she had not seen the woman last night, perhaps she could get up like previous mornings, appear without a word by the teapot, and if Ma told her that it would be better if she wore her black skirt for tonight's gathering, say nothing but *all right.* But now that she had seen the woman and had seen the red, ripe apples, Ma's grumblings had become strangely meaningless to her. Her voice had evolved into an annoying high-pitch noise that even if she covered her ears, still penetrated the bone and skin of her hands and found its way into the narrow passageway, so that gradually she felt that the noise came from inside her ears or the same old words bounced back against the little drum and echoed over and over, preaching to her about matters that she just didn't understand. The problem was exactly that she just did not understand anymore. She did not even understand the red Persian cashmere on the wall anymore, nor the narrow-necked blue pot from Esfahan[4] with the fish design. Now that she thought about it, she actually realized that in fact she had never quite

[3] In Iran, it is customary to have peddlers that trade salt for dried-out bread.

[4] A city in Iran, best known for its historical monuments and Islamic art.

understood. Even in those childhood years when she stood up by Grandma's side and imitated her praying moves. Merely since these things were always there, she had imagined that they had to always be there. Or perhaps somehow she needed them to be there, to give harmony to the doings and sayings and hours. A harmony that had the calmness of Grandma's home in it. But now that she had found the woman, she realized that it was more real to her than anything else that she had ever assumed to be real: the peace of Grandma's home, or the red cashmere, or the morning tea, or the *khorshid khanooms*, or even Tehran. Or even herself.

Ma's distant voice disturbed her train of thoughts. She was asking something, but her words were no longer comprehensible. She rubbed her chest. It was covered in sweat from the heat. For the thousandth time she told herself that it was spring already and covering up with such a heavy blanket in this temperature was insanity. If Ma had not taken the blanket out, there was no way . . .She kicked the blanket away and let her thighs cool. She remembered the bareness of the woman, the curvature of her thighs and her waist and the two suspended apples. . .and she saw his questioning eyes in front of her and the crack on the wall that was like a snake. . .and her hands that involuntarily grabbed his hands and. . .no she really had no choice. This time, she got up.

She stood by the mirror and with a quick look made sure one more time that the door was closed. She gently pulled the light dress up and took it off. Her heart started pounding. No, she was not mistaken. No, they were right there, in her loins, ripe and red, ripe and. . .a moment of hesitation. Frightened, she leaped and pulled the blinds' rope. Blinds closed. The rope rubbed against her bare thigh. She smiled and her mouth filled with the taste of bitter almonds.

"We should have a small ceremony for the anniversary of Grandma's death. . . ." Terrified she turned towards the voice and bent over to cover her bareness. The black of her pupils had filled the white of her eyes. Her mother was standing by the door, with Grandma's flowery praying veil in her hands.

* * *

She ran into the kitchen. Grandma was singing for her: *My girl is demure, my girl is beautiful, I won't give her to just anyone, I won't show her to just anyone. . . .*[5] Rising up on her toes, she reached for and grabbed another fistful of plums from the bowl on the kitchen counter and jammed it into her cheeks, wiped her hands with her dress and ran onto the mosaics barefoot. As she opened the door, she heard Grandma's voice from behind: "You little imp, the indecency, half-naked you run into the al—" The chilly wind that blew in the narrow alley, in the shade of the trees, crawled under her summer dress.

[5] Translation of an Iranian folk song, usually sung to unmarried young women or little girls.

Autopsy

Sarah Cross

Blood, not sickled now,
but crimson, rolling over sepia skin
pooled, filled the alleys of the table.

Lungs full of rain
were yellow at the edges.
Freed from its bloody
pericardial cocoon,
open ventricular doors revealed
no clot in the heart.
Each kidney was a seahorse
in its thick skin.
32 hundred grams of liver,
wet brick, broken.
The pearl of the pituitary was exposed
in its dark cell, then cut out.

Less than one day dead,
he was my age exactly.
No one cried,
as his body was cut apart,
little reverence for the delicacy
which put it together
warm dark cell by wet cell.
When we went down later to remove
the rest of his vertebral
column—cracked kindling breaking,
both bags had been opened,
betraying a farewell visit.

Some day I may have to say:
I cannot save you.
I will help you move quietly.

Returning the Rent-a-Baby

Brock Dethier

I carry my cancer 'cross campus
like a baby.
It brings the women around.
They coo endearments
with softened eyes,
finger my shoulder,
laugh sadly.

"Rent a baby
Get a babe."
Thursday through Sunday, a booth on the quad,
babies by the minute,
black, white, or Asian,
paper or plastic,
identical onesies
for mid-date baby exchange.

Guys buy an hour
to parade on the library steps.
A babied stroll through the union
makes the lassies swoon.
Heated drop-off box
behind Family Life
for late-date convenience.

A franchise on every campus,
website rimmed with faces
lured by leased love, borrowed beneficence.
Available in "Rip," who sleeps
through earthquaking orgasms,
"Coo," the cuddly conversation starter, and
"Poopy," for those attracted to a helpless man
and a baby in need.

My baby talks already.
It says, "You made me,
but I am not you.
You will die so I can grow.
I am your punishment and your curse,
the fruit of your excess.
Yet you have loved me all your life."

I want to return this baby,
this pus-filled pomegranate.
Sympathy is a shallow grave.
Everybody loves a guy with cancer
because it's not them.
I've had enough of such love.

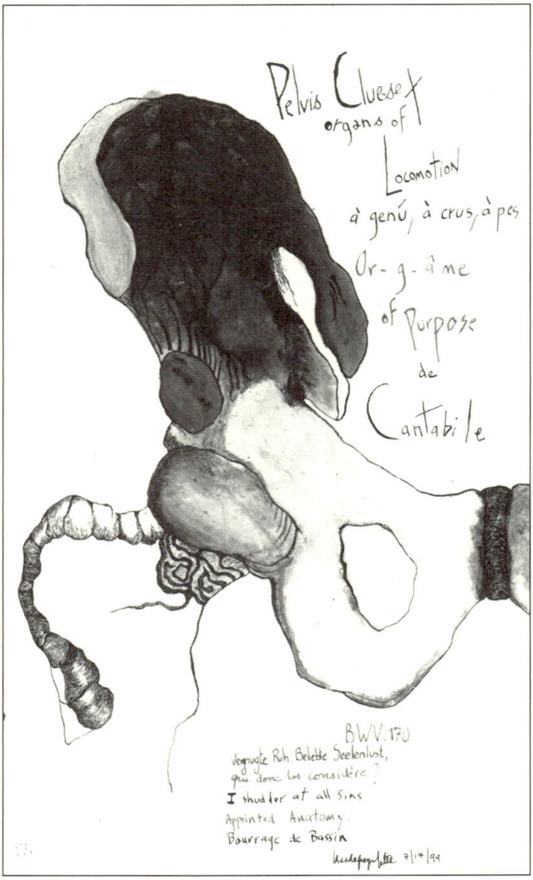

Nicole Peyrafitte ~ Cantata *BWV170*

My Brother's Life: No Double-Blind Study

Susan Luzzaro

My brother Richard developed a faith in drugs far deeper than the faith he once had in the Lutheran God. In the church of drugs there are, as in any other place of worship, abasement, ecstasy, and the possibility of redemption. The psychiatrist doubles well for the priest with the small, white wafer in his extended hand. Though my brother likes to talk about pigeons, both living and dead, the majority of his conversation is about his meds. For thirty-five years he has sat in a circle with other lost sheep and learned the catechism of staying on his medication. The litany needs to be chanted daily as many stop taking their prescriptions because of the dangerous and unpleasant side effects. When my brother and I talked about his meds, the discussion resembled that of a biblical scholar searching for evidence of God; he had faith that one day a miracle drug would resurrect the infinitely possible self that he was when he was born.

The drugs were destroying Richard, but I was slow to understand that he could or should be rescued from them. After my parents died, tragically and almost simultaneously, my husband and I inherited the care of Richard. Born normal, he experienced a high fever at the age of two and was diagnosed retarded. At the onset of adolescence, he behaved in an increasingly aggressive manner; finally my parents relinquished him to halfway houses, state hospitals, and board and care homes. Layered onto the diagnosis of retarded was the diagnosis of schizophrenia. For a long time I was preoccupied with the tragedy of my parents' deaths and Richard was tended to more by "the system" than by my husband and me. We would pick him up every three weeks and take him out to dinner. On Christmas and Thanksgiving he spent the night. That was it; that was the extent of what we could do.

When we picked Richard up to spend the night, his board and care home would give us a plastic grocery bag filled with his meds. Like a large passenger, the bag occupied an entire seat. The meds come in monthly punch out cards marked a.m., Noon, 5:00, and p.m. At the apogee of his prescribed medication he was taking: 250 mg of Depakote six times a day for mood swings; 125 mg of Serentil four times a day for antipsychotic behavior; 300 mg of Clozaril two times a day for antipsychotic behavior; 2 mg of Benzotropine four times a day to counteract the side effects of the other drugs (Benzotropine has a slew of its own of side effects); 150 mg of Bupropion six times a day, an antidepressant to help him quit smoking though he had given up trying; 10 mg of Trazadone for sleep; and 1 mg of Ativan as needed for anxiety. He also received a shot of Depo-Provera once a week to keep him from sexually acting out, though he had committed only modest and unverified offenses.

Very few studies address the safety or efficacy of polypharmacy. It stands to reason that given the many drugs available to treat schizophrenia, testing all of the possible combinations would be difficult. There is also extremely limited research on the effects of psychotropics on the developmentally disabled population. My brother's records indicate that he was hospitalized several times for medication toxicity. One entry reads as follows: "Psychiatric unit decided that swelling in legs was a side effect of medications (Risperdal, Inderal and Mellaril and Congentin were discontinued)."

Richard was first put on Thorazine when he was twelve. Born in l951, perhaps he was ordained for drugs one way or another. According to Robert Whitaker, whose book *Mad In America* exhaustively researches treatment of the mentally ill, "By l970, more than fifty percent of mentally retarded children in America were being drugged." From the time Richard was first given Thorazine, he has never, until recently, envisioned a life without drugs. Like a twentieth-century son of Frankenstein, he is pieced together by pink, yellow, and white pills.

The San Diego board and care home where Richard lives houses sixteen men. Sometimes, in a convenient and economical attempt to keep the men groomed, the caregiver gets out the electric shaver and shears their heads. Even though the intentions are good, whenever I came to pick my brother up and found his head shaved, I couldn't help but be upset. The fact that a shaved head has become a popular style surprises me as it evokes so many negative associations: concentration camps, boot camp, electroshock therapy, lobotomy, head lice and so on. My brother is six feet tall and weighed, until recently, 220 pounds. When his head is shaved, it highlights the fact that his head is so much smaller than his body. It's like accessorizing lunacy. When we enter restaurants, or museums, or wherever we go on our outings, people keep a wary distance and try to restrain their children from commenting.

My brother's deterioration was marked by many signs. He would fall asleep on our way to or from restaurants. He became obese. He developed asthma and eczema. He lost his balance easily and had a series of bad falls. He was unable to hold his urine and had to be put on Ditropan. His front teeth darkened and one by one his back teeth began to be pulled. His tongue rolled around involuntarily in his mouth and his hands stiffened and convulsed. He had to be tested every week for a deadly blood disease called agranulosis and monthly for diabetes, which several of the men in his board and care home had already developed.

There was something tragically sweet about Richard's attitude in the face of these ravages; he was like a five-year-old who had already intuited the immense indifference of the universe. In the same way that he let go of his hair or teeth without complaint, he seemed resigned to giving away his person piecemeal. Once when I asked him about a health problem he was having, he said simply, "Just a few tears, Sue, don't worry about me." Although I was bothered by my brother's appearance, I had only a deep sense of complacency about his condition. Brain damage was forever. Schizophrenia was incurable. His problems were too big, too technical, too sad. The best I could do was apply the Band-Aid of an outing, the balm of pizza.

On one trip home Richard told me he was going to have another tooth pulled. There was a rare lull in my over full life so I called the dentist's office to plead for his tooth. I mistakenly thought it had to do with his being a Medicare patient; I imagined that it was cheaper to pull than to fill. The receptionist told me, "There's nothing we can do. We treat a lot of patients on antipsychotics. Inevitably, the antipsychotics will cause him to lose all of his teeth."

That was the first time anyone had connected for me a specific deterioration in my brother related to his drugs. With a little research, I found that dry mouth, or xerostemia, is the side effect of many antipsychotics.

One discovery led to another. Many of his other problems were side effects as well. Clozaril can cause not only agranulosis but also incontinence; it has a black box warning for heart inflammation or myocarditis. The tongue rolling, "tardive dyskinesia," has been linked to permanent changes in the brain and a higher mortality rate, is irreversible, and is a side effect of almost all antipsychotics. The new generation of antipsychotics appears to be equally implicated. Additionally, many of his drugs cause serious weight gain, which aggravates the likelihood of diabetes.

Richard attends behavioral day programs where he is assigned a psychiatrist. I called the psychiatrist who had been attending to my brother for many years and spoke to him about my fears. Rather casually he asked me how old my brother was and how long he had been on antipsychotics. Then, equally casually, he told me I should expect this kind of decline, that the drugs were taking their toll.

Perhaps too late, I realized I should do something.

Madness Museum

The quality of life in the halfway houses and board and care homes where Richard has lived has varied. Clients in the houses are there for different reasons. Some have criminal records, some are rehabilitating—or not—from street drugs, some are schizophrenic, some abandoned, some mentally ill or impaired. They are all boxed together.

In one home Richard often found hypodermic needles in the bathroom. In that same place, he had one of his breakdowns that landed him in the hospital. The breakdown was belatedly attributed to the random way my brother was given his meds. Ultimately, I was told that the house manager was swallowing his clients' drugs. The house manager died from cirrhosis shortly after my brother was hospitalized.

Richard had another breakdown when he lived in a tiny, hot hotel that had been converted into a halfway house. With a damaged brain, a belly full of drugs, and a small monthly paycheck, he was supposed to find his way from halfway to whole. One day he threw his broken TV into the middle of a four-lane street in front of the hotel and was sent to county mental health where I found him tied to a chair. His wrists and ankles were bloody from the ties around them. He was heavily drugged, yet he kept trying to stand, forgetting that he was tied up. My mind has blocked out anything else about the day. Did I complain, or did I somehow think it was part of my brother's condition, his treatment?

Another time, my brother got angry and threw a lamp through a plate glass window. This time he was sent to a state hospital where only the hardened mentally ill were sent. He told me recently (and he may have told me before, but I wasn't paying attention) that when he was in the state hospital, he was kept in solitary confinement for two weeks. Most people would be angry. Richard was simply resigned. "The only people I saw were the guards who came in to feed me. That's wrong, Sue, because you're not supposed to be alone for so long."

During all of these incidents, including the hospitalization, my brother was being treated with antipsychotics. It never occurred to me to ask when these medications were going to cure him, or to question why he should continue to take them when they obviously weren't working. I was blind, too, to the fact that many of his "psychotic breakdowns" coincided with what might be argued unnecessary med changes, changes that were a result of new drugs becoming available.

Antipsychotics have been the dominant way of treating schizophrenics since the 1950's, and perhaps the side effects look harmless compared to the things that my brother would have had to endure had he been born in another era. He did not have to suffer the swinging chair, the spinning bed, bloodletting, ice water baths, insulin or shock treatments, or a lobotomy. If these treatments were arranged chronologically, in sequential museum rooms, from the vantage point of history, we might see them as follies of another age, laughable if they were not tragic. Certainly, it would be clear to us how inhumane and experimental such treatments were.

The World Health Organization in two separate studies has found that schizophrenics in underdeveloped countries have a far better chance of recovery than in the United States. One of the factors that was different in the underdeveloped countries is that patients were put on fewer drugs for a markedly more limited time.

Experience and research taken together, it's possible to think that my brother, and many like him, are living in the last exhibit room of the Madness Museum. In one corner there is a board and care diorama. It's early in the evening and the caregivers have already dispensed the bedtime meds. The clients are sitting on a dilapidated couch in stoned silence staring at a fuzzy TV. Many of them are obese, in varying stages of diabetes, and have uncontrollable facial tics, lolling tongues and stiff limbs. In the other corner, separated by a wall, there might be a young man or woman in a dark suit with a briefcase full of sample drugs engaged in a discussion with a psychiatrist. The sales rep is speaking about an informative all expense-paid conference in Hawaii.

If the Diagnosis Fits, Wear It

Psychiatrists are assigned to my brother through his outpatient mental health program. I contacted the psychiatrist who had been treating my brother for about ten years; he agreed to meet with me and discuss my brother's medication. He reluctantly agreed to remove the Depo-Provera shot from my brother's regime and to begin a reduction of his medication. The psychiatrist worked closely with the board and care manager, and it is my contention that board and care managers prefer to have clients as medicated as possible. Shortly after the Depo-Provera was discontinued, the board and care manager reported to the doctor that my brother was making sexually aggressive remarks, which almost led to his being put back on the shot. I contacted his sheltered workshop and found out that the remark was "Hello, beautiful."

Another complaint from the home about Richard "staring" resulted in his having Zyprexa, yet another antipsychotic, layered onto his medication. This antipsychotic has a higher link with diabetes than many others. I phoned his psychiatrist and told him, "I have looked up the side effects of Zyprexa. Perhaps you don't realize that we have a family history of diabetes. Richard's grandfather died of diabetes. His aunt and uncle also suffer from diabetes."

"I'm aware of Richard's history," he said.

"Then do you think this is the right drug for him?" I persisted. He hung up on me. He later told my brother that he hung up on me because I was rude.

Richard was aware of his own deterioration and was enthusiastic about changing psychiatrists. The meeting with the new psychiatrist took place at a large, square table that allowed a safe distance between us. Richard was at my side, his own best advocate. The new psychiatrist, the therapist, and the nurse were aligned on the other side of the table. I had also requested the program manager of the behavioral clinic to attend, and he positioned himself neutrally. Still, the tension was palpable.

Because there are no blood or biological tests for establishing that someone has schizophrenia, and the DSM does not seek to understand the etiology of the illness but simply groups the mentally ill according to behavior, my first question was about Richard's diagnosis.

It had been years since Richard had acted erratically. I was beginning to wonder if he might have been misdiagnosed or if, with age, the schizophrenia had lessened or subsided. I also mentioned that the last thorough examination of Richard had not been able to distinguish between schizophrenia and depression. Nevertheless, the psychiatrist stated that my brother had schizo-affective disorder, which was characterized by mood swings, hallucinations, and delusions. I asked everyone at the table when was the last time they had seen my brother behave in a delusional way. No one at the table had ever witnessed my brother have a hallucination, and Richard chimed in saying, "I never hear voices."

The counselor thought she remembered that Richard had received messages from the radio some years before. (I thought it best not to mention that we all receive messages from the radio.) She said that she would attempt to re-contact the counselor who was working with Richard at that time. The nurse, who has often been Richard's advocate, brought the discussion to a head by saying he had not witnessed Richard exhibiting any of this behavior in the five years he had been attending the behavioral clinic.

The team resolved to re-evaluate Richard's diagnosis, but more importantly, to begin immediately to reduce his medication. It was a victory fraught with worrisome possibilities, and I felt the heaviness of responsibility, but Richard was ecstatic. His survival, to the extent that he has survived, comes from his ability to transform a piece of straw into a bale of hay, a shred of hope into a reason to live.

I accepted the part I had to play in my brother's recovery—in recovering my brother. It wasn't enough to simply reduce the drugs. I needed to un-abandon him. I needed to reintegrate him into family life, community life. I have heard about studies where children suffering from attention deficit syndrome were calmed, were slowed, by the color green, by grass and trees and park-like surroundings. Richard's drug-induced torpor, smoke-filled ambiance, needed to be pierced by blades of green, blue horizons, the important idea of a world, and the constancy of people who love him.

The Efficacy of Love

I have a picture of Richard at a Mexican restaurant celebrating his birthday two years ago. My husband, my children, and my children's children are seated around the table. We are animated by margaritas, sodas, and mariachi music. We make toasts to Richard and attempt to sing *Happy Birthday* over the background noise, but he is nodding off. He is fat, bald, and when I take his picture his eyes flicker open, hover between sleep and song. He wakes periodically and there is a desperate quality to the way he eats—not with pleasure, but like an animal who is afraid his kill will be stolen. He had already downed a basket of chips, and, when his food arrives, he brings his mouth close to the plate so the fork acts almost a straw. He sucks down thousands of calories—beans, burritos, tacos, enchiladas, then dozes off again. My daughter quietly comments that he looks worse than ever. She is trying to prepare me.

One year later, as we amble down the sensuous aisles of Whole Foods Market, Richard pushes the grocery cart beside me like a husband. Though the casual observer might not see it, compared to that picture two years ago, Richard glows like the statue of David. He has lost about twenty-five pounds. I have replaced his sweatpants with elastic waist cords and he wears his hair in a short shag. His antipsychotics have been cut in half, and continue to be reduced 25 milligrams each month. There are always a few rough days after the reduction, but he is doing so well even his psychiatrist has commented on how often Richard smiles now. He is alert and aware of his alertness; he savors the world he is returning to. We praise the strawberries, sample the fig bread, and toothpick small squares of cheese. He blows my cool in this cool place, but my cart and, at the risk of bathos, my heart, are too full to care. He is an experiment in reverse. Instead of finding out how many drugs he can tolerate, we are finding out how few he needs. There is still the danger of relapse, but I choose to think of what's around the next corner in terms of *creme fraiche* or green olives.

The pleasures of domesticity are not lost on Richard, either. As he positions the flour in the corner of the cart, he says to me "Sue, what would you think if I told you I might settle down and get married?" I don't tell him my fears or the odds against him. I let his words stand for hope.

Kathleen Gunton ~ *Dancing Iris*

Birth/Rebirth

Terri Brown-Davidson

To curl up in a Lotus.
What a paradox. A conundrum.
There's nothing fetal about a Lotus.
The embryo, red-rinsed,
luxuriates in wombwarmed languor,
anticipating a birth struggle
unredolent with "Carpe Diems"
or theories of Eternal Recurrence.
I shift my forehead closer
to the dustpocked dojo floor.
My thighs evince a strain that sings
of sweetly snapping ligaments,
of bones brutally shifted from sockets
though rebirth's not a birthright.
A fresh soul's what I long for.

Barbara Nevaldine ~ *Bloodroot*

Nicole Peyrafitte ~ *Cantata BWV18*

Wherever You Are

Joyce Holmes McAllister

—for SG

Do they have macaroni and cheese,
the kind you like, top crust
a deep gold, a little crisp, and
underneath, the macaroni
firm but soft to the bite,
the taste of sharp cheese
melted on your tongue?

And hot dogs, Hebrew National,
religiously safe, Jewish mother fattening—
are they marching around together
almost naked, rolls askew, relish dripping,
mustard sliding down their middles,
miniature yellow rivers on the run?
And do you eat one, sometimes two,
like you used to do?

Does someone cook potato pancakes,
and do they make a batch for you,
sputtering in the skillet, ragged edges
curling brown, potato, onion, matzo meal;
do you eat them, every one, hot and
topped with applesauce or sour cream
and then lie restless all night long
from indigestion, latke dreams?

Today I curled my mind around the taste
of early corn and waited for your call,
forgetting it would never come again.
"How do you cook corn on the cob?"
Maybe I should holler into space,
"Not in a microwave—on the stove,
boiling water, five minutes, like every year."
Can you hear me, wherever you are?

Yolanda Tooley ~ *Harmonica*

The Red Ribbon

Vishwas R. Gaitonde

South Indians drink their "filter coffee" with a devotion verging on worship. The whole act is a consecrated ritual that starts with the selection of the finest, ripest coffee beans that are ground finely into earthy brown dust, which is then brewed in a small, hour-glass-shaped metal kettle that has an upper and lower compartment with a filter in between.

So when an entrepreneur duo opened a chain of cafés in Chennai, the largest city in Southern India and the bastion of the South Indian coffee drinker, people shook their heads knowingly and deprecatingly, feeling sorry for the poor devils who had sunk their money into such a foolhardy venture.

But the old guard had not reckoned on how many youngsters would joyfully convert to the new religion, with no effort on the part of the missionaries. The converts had read about the cafés on the sidewalks of Paris, the coffee parlors of London, and the coffee shops that dot America from Boston to San Diego. An air ticket to these countries was out of their reach, but an evening with friends at The Chic Coffee Corner Shoppe was certainly affordable. Now a piece of America was within their grasp, even if it was a make-believe America. They could now taste what the Americans tasted and even revel in American sounds: MTV blasted from television sets mounted randomly in the café, and there was the whoosh-whoosh-whoosh of the large metal coffee machines working overtime behind the bar counter.

It was a Saturday evening, the busiest time of the week for the cafés. Each store in the chain was situated on a street corner, and the walls that faced the street were made of thick tinted glass. The coffee drinkers could look onto the street as the city lights sprang to life in the fading twilight and at the maze of vehicle headlamps on the road when the traffic became snarled as more people joined the ones out there for shopping or revelry.

Those on the street could look into the packed cafés where people bunched up at the entrance waiting for a table. They eyed the people sitting on the gleaming chromium barstools, and on the chairs, which were upholstered with the same dazzling, garish red vinyl as the barstools. The wooden tables were a pale brown, the color of weak and very milky coffee. Fluorescent tube lights set beneath silver metal plaques encased in the false ceiling cast an abrasive, discordant white light over everyone and everything.

The lines did not deter others from joining them; the urge to be part of the in-crowd was strong. As they stood in resigned patience, they watched the noisy crowd: the teenagers in their faded jeans and crumpled T-shirts, the more daring boys sporting an earring or a bandana (to keep up the illusion of a pretend America, one had to dress as Americans did), other young men and women conventionally dressed in shirts and pants, skirts, saris, and *salwar-kameezes*. Scattered sporadically among these animated groups were older men and women affecting, at least for an hour of the evening, that they had found their second youth.

Those who waited for a table continuously scanned the room and so were the first to notice the small commotion in the center of the café that was certainly not part of the general bustle. A group of women sitting there looked angrily at each other, but their most menacing stares were directed at a plump woman in a light blue sari who was tearfully pleading with them.

Without warning, two of the other women yanked the woman in the blue sari to her feet and forcefully shoved her away from them. She staggered between the tables, dropping the pastry she had been eating and quickly extending her hand to steady herself and avoid crashing into the people at the adjoining tables. She made as though to rejoin the group but was stopped in her tracks when one of the ladies who had pushed her lashed out in a stentorian voice: "Get out of this place at once—and don't ever try to meet us again. It is finished—all finished—understand?" And then under her breath, "You foul, filthy creature."

"But I have done nothing wrong!" The attacked woman's response was a cry of anguish, of baffled incomprehension. Once again she tried to move back to the group, and once again a barricade of angry stares repulsed her. Then the lady who had spoken before, a small lady with short hair cut in a wedge down to the nape of the neck, a petite, aggressive dragon with eyes that sent out sparks of brimstone, lashed out again.

"You are HIV positive. You have no place with us, no place here among these people. Go away or we will throw you out, dear—or get the manager to do it."

As the altercation built up, one head after another turned in their direction and one voice after another hushed. The television, which had been loud, became deafening. At the last sharp comment, a pall of shocked solemnity descended on the packed café as though a wand had been waved darkly, a spell of black magic cast. Then, all of a sudden, somebody silenced all the television sets, accentuating the spell.

The manager suddenly appeared before the angry ladies. The uncertain expression on his youthful face and the way he shifted his weight from one foot to the other marked him out as a greenhorn.

"I can't throw her out, she is a human being too." He started out uneasily, then suddenly added with a spurt of confidence, "As long as she can pay her bill, she is okay."

"She isn't paying the bill, we are." The dragon lady was sarcastic. "We just found out that she is HIV positive—that means AIDS, you know that, don't you—and the woman has been happily sipping from my cup. Don't you think you should throw her out before she messes up things some more for your other patrons?"

A lanky young man who was sitting at the adjoining table with two others suddenly rose to his full height—a good six feet—and snapped at the dragon lady in an irate voice loud enough to bounce off the glass walls of the room, "What do you mean, behaving like this? Have you any idea how many people in this room are HIV positive?"

Immediately the distressed lady ran up to him, sobbing, "Please help me, sir." Three tears dribbled down a cheek. "Please help me, I don't know what to do now."

Now the man was at a loss, moving a step back as though he was afraid that the sobbing lady would clutch on to him. His two companions stared into their coffee cups intently. The air vibrated with interpersonal electricity. The man suddenly looked angry again, but as he was about to speak, the dragon lady cut in forcefully.

"Chill it, chill it everybody! What you have been watching is not a real event but a fake one. We're from a non-profit organization called Arygrec that works for AIDS awareness. In case you don't know it, today is World AIDS Day, and we thought this was an excellent way to get your attention."

She got everybody's attention, but the voltage in the air dissipated rapidly as people turned back to their coffee and conversations again. The women went from table to table distributing folded red ribbons and offering to answer any queries people might have about AIDS. Nobody expected another interruption that evening, yet they got one.

A small man, pale and crinkled, with pastel pink cheeks, bald as a mushroom and with a blonde goatee beard, who had thus far been hidden behind a newspaper, suddenly stood up and burst into exposition, waving his coffee spoon in the air as his eyes darted behind his gold-rimmed glasses.

"C'est merveilleux. C'est tout a fait ahurrissant! J'avais renoncé tout espoir pour ce pays miserable. Je l'avais abandonné comme un bordel, un bordel absolu des crétins...une grande foule des aveugles, des stupides et des êtres ignorant étant dévorés vif par SIDA et par leur stupidité totale."

The steady pattering in a language nobody understood made heads turn again; the atmosphere became surreal once more. A pretend American café had truly turned foreign now. The little Frenchman—or was he Canadian?—strutted like a proud cockerel up to the young man who had defended the lady.

The young man had been as much at a loss as the others at the French chatter, picking up a few words that were familiar to him—*cretins, stupides, ignorant, SIDA*—as his mind scrambled to piece together the possible meaning. The Frenchman picked up a red ribbon from the table and gallantly pinned it on the man's shirt, continuing to declaim in his swinging cadence more incomprehensible words: *"Mais jusqu'il y a des jeunes gens courageux comme eux, si ce n'est pas un incident unique, si les jeunes se levent et prennent des mesures, alors y encore expoir pour l'Inde. En fait, il y a l'espoir. Ça se sent si bien, ah oui, vraiment ça se sent."*

The red ribbon stood out prominently against his light yellow shirt. He could not bring himself to remove it right after it had been pinned on, not in front of others. His friends kept snickering and passing snide remarks on his chivalry—gallantry that had seemed noble just a moment ago but now became an object of fun to his friends when the heroic knight had been converted into a clown, the hapless victim of a set-up. He knew that their teasing was good natured and all in a friendly spirit, but he kept the red ribbon pinned on his shirt in defiance of their jests. He slurped up his coffee quickly, said his goodbyes, and left.

He rode down the city streets on his motorbike, going a little faster than he should. The wind fanned his face vigorously but instead of cooling him down, he could feel his cheeks warm up and then burn as he relived the evening in his mind. When the lady in the blue sari had been so unfairly targeted, he had spoken up in the heat of the moment, flushed and spurred by emotion, not thinking of where his words might lead him. As he spoke, he saw different kinds of mute admiration in the eyes of the people around him. When the charade was revealed, amusement replaced the approbation in their eyes, but he could see some esteem for him persisted—after all, he had acted before anybody had realized that it was a show. But then that little goat of a Frenchman had pinned the red ribbon on his chest as though it was a medal for courage, a badge of honor. The Frenchman's eyes were twinkling as he did so—but he saw mockery, not appreciation.

What did the Frenchman see in him? Was there something in his manner, in his stance, in the way he spoke, that had given away the fact that he was a weakling? He wondered, as he swerved to negotiate a particularly crooked street. The indignity that the lady had suffered today in the café—and of course, she was only pretending to suffer—the indignity, even had it been real, was nothing compared to what his mother was subjected to every day. He had boldly attacked the petite dragon lady in public and yet shied away from confronting his father in private. He swore mightily when his mother showed him her welts and blotchy bruises but was struck dumb when the lord, master, and tyrant he had been brought up to fear and obey walked into the room. His mother would urge him to hold back his temper, and he would cravenly comply.

He could never defy, would never stand up to his father—the man who devised a devilish new way each day to be beastly to his mother. The first time he had tried, it had ended in a fiasco.

"As long as you stay under my roof and eat my food, you have no right to put on your arrogant airs and tell me what to do." His father smiled thinly, his amusement stretching his lips. "If you don't like it here, you are free to leave. The door is always open. Your mother can always visit you, even live with you for short periods if she wishes to." His father's smile broadened.

He clenched his fist in helplessness. He did not make enough money to be able to rent an apartment and run an independent household. He had sent out his resumes so many times in his quest for a higher paying job that the act of mailing them out now became mechanical and meaningless. Many had not even been acknowledged; none had resulted in an interview. In his parents' house he did not have to pay rent and he got his meals, which meant that with his salary he could ride a motorbike, wear nice clothes, and hang out with his friends at the coffee shop or occasionally at one of the local bars.

But then he could do nothing to help his mother, especially when she didn't want him to talk about it to anybody. They had to maintain the appearance of a happy family; no girl would marry the son of a man who was known as a wife-beater. "If you plant carrot seeds, you cannot expect peas to sprout. Like father, like son," they would say and look elsewhere for a match for their daughters.

Sometimes he fantasized that a rich wife would be his way out, that his mother could then leave his father and live with them—or that the mere threat of that would jolt his father enough to change his brutish ways. But rich girls only married poor boys in the movies, and then they had all kinds of bizarre problems before they got to the point where they could live happily ever after.

Today for the first time in his life, he had accumulated the courage—he didn't know how he did what he did, but he had felt a new elation as he was doing it. For the first time, he had felt like a man, had felt some kind of fulfillment—and then the bubble had burst savagely. It was all a sham, and he had been reduced to nothing, back to what he was and perhaps always would be. Of all the people in the café, only the Frenchman—whoever he was and whatever he was doing in this corner of India—only the Frenchman had seen through him and openly embarrassed him by branding him with the scarlet ribbon.

When he reached his house, he parked his motorbike carefully and tiptoed indoors through the back door. The kitchen light was not on, but he could hear sniffles come from within. His mother was sobbing again in the dark. He stood still, then carefully unpinned the red ribbon from his shirt and flicked it into the garbage can where it joined the potato peels, soggy coffee grains, broken eggshells, and the leftovers of the previous day's dinner.

That Was Then: Growing Up in Rural South Carolina

Anetha Frasier
Dearing Writing Award, First Place
Faculty/Employee Division

There are many forms of separation. It exists not only between the races, but within the races as well. I experienced at least two kinds of separation while growing up in Nesmith, South Carolina, during the 1970's and '80s.

Although blacks and whites lived in that rural community, the closest we came to socializing was if our properties aligned or when we exchanged short greetings in passing. The only time a black person set foot in white folks' houses was in a domestic capacity. And whites never set foot in black-owned homes. When passing, it is expected that you will speak (or you would be considered disrespectful by both races) and even exchange small talk, but you don't stop to hold any conversations.

Scattered throughout the city were five convenience stores, four places for men to get drunk, and two candy shacks. The Pump House, Ventice's Shop, The Red Door, and the local ABC were the favored spots for alcoholic consumption; they were the establishments that only blacks patronized. The Pump House was the most popular and was considered a "den of iniquity" and a blight on the reputation of the community. It was a place where men went to get drunk and whatever else was available for entertainment. I say men because no woman who valued her good name would be caught dead there! Its popularity was the downfall of many marriages and quite a few families. More than one effort was made on the part of good citizens to close that particular establishment to no avail. In fact, it is still in operation today. Two of the convenience stores were frequented by whites; the other establishments were for blacks only.

There were three churches. All the white people in community went to the one on the hill, and the African American population worshipped at either one of the other two or some church elsewhere. There was one post office everyone used with a very nosy postmistress who steamed opened people's mail. There was one school in the vicinity that accommodated children from daycare through the twelfth grade. None of the white children attended. Their parents got up each morning to take them to schools in neighboring cities. The white man who lived four houses down from us had a son my age, but I only knew that through my parents because I never saw him. I used to find it amazing that although blacks and whites did not socialize each knew the other's business. If by chance you got to ask anyone of any racial distinction about his or her neighbor, they could tell you something. Apparently, gossip transcends color lines with no problem. Even today, though much has changed, that much still holds true in Nesmith.

However, since blacks and whites lived such segregated existences on a social level, a great part of my early memories comes from the black part of the community. It was as if the idealism of the Atlanta Compromise was being realized right there in little old Nesmith. I do not recall anyone protesting the situation or doing anything about it. That was just the way it was. There is no reason to challenge a situation if everyone seems content with it.

Another form of separation existed in that little city that had nothing to do with skin color and much to do with socioeconomic circumstances. The haves and have-nots. We were considered one of the have-nots. It was not necessary for me to go to the newly integrated school to feel what it was like to be shunned for no other reason than who I was. That could be found in Nesmith and at the local school.

There were black families in certain parts of the community who were quite well off and liked everyone to know it. Their children were pains in the butt to go to school with. My sisters and I went through a long period in the early days of isolation from the other students. Until we found allies and the inner strength to deal with those people, we were subjected to a lot of vicious teasing. Of course, having a father who was "street happy" and who more readily gave his hard-earned money to the Pump House than his family did not help matters at all. As a matter of fact, it accounted for most of our problems. If your daddy (and sometimes your mommy) were known to frequent such places, you were in for it at school. I noticed though that most of the teasing came from the older kids; the younger ones just went along with it because it was easier than defying the older ones.

There were five girls in our house (four sisters and one cousin). There were no boys in my family. Our household also included my mother, father, and our maternal grandmother. One cold morning my mother got us out of bed to get ready for school with the usual scolding because we were once again running late. Everyone was vying for a place in front of the heater, trying to get to the bathroom first, blaming someone else for something missing, accusing someone of taking something that belonged to someone else, and my mother in the middle of it all telling us for the hundredth time,"Y'all betta git ya 'hinds outa here and catch that bus 'cause nobody got no money ta waste on gas ta take y'all to school when the bus stops right in ya mouth."

Normally, I was dressed first and would go to the lane to keep watch for the bus. As it approached, I would yell back as it got to each lane before ours. My two youngest sisters were habitually the last to come scrambling from the house. We would laugh and talk at the lane until the bus came to our stop. All talk and laughter ceased when we got on the bus. We could only just wonder what we would have to deal with that day.

I was last to get on. I found an empty seat and sat down. The next stop was where the trouble began. It came in the form of Doreen (a ninth grader at the time) and her younger cousins. Everyone called her Reena; I called her "Nasty Bat." Sandra sat down next to me. The first thing that went through my mind was, "Oh God, why me?" The bus got quiet because I knew, as did everyone else, Reena would have something to say. She did. I don't remember her ugly words, but I do remember her ugly actions. She took one of her books and carefully slid it between Sandra and me, being cautious not to touch me in case something (I do not know what that something was) rubbed off me onto her or Sandra. The whole bus burst out laughing. I just turned away and stared unseeing out the window, willing the bus ride to be over soon and hoping the bus floor would open up so Nasty Bat could drop through on her way down to where she belonged. As disgusting as she was, Doreen was only one of many who treated us that way.

As I said, we learned to deal with it in our own way. I buried myself in books, art, and the local PBS station. The sister under me was our wild child, but she managed, with our help, to rein herself in. The youngest two were social butterflies but polar opposites in scholastic achievement. Despite our many differences, we had much in common: for us, family always comes first in our loyalties; thanks to our mother, we are all strong believers in faith; and, finally, we have learned to agree to disagree whenever we cannot agree.

Today, I believe I can say our family has succeeded. Many of those same people became our friends in later years. Oh and Doreen? Well, she definitely became a better person to be around, especially since we were the only ones in the community that would have anything to do with her at times. It is ironic that the devices we used to work through those early days are what sustain us now through troubled times. Those devices include calling on each other, praying, reassessing situations, shopping (for my sisters), reading (for me), and just writing it down sometimes. Yes, we have all grown up and are now living separate lives, but we will always be close partly because of those early days of separation in rural South Carolina.

Disbelief
After the chemo

Andrea Potos

It makes no sense, my sister and I agree—
my aunt's hair and fingernails growing back thick
and luxurious, her skin reclaiming
its former sheen, her eyelashes becoming
long and dark again,
while inside her body, the renegade cells
complete the dirty work the doctors assert
is a done deal, though secretly
I disbelieve, I dare them to defy this radiance, this life.

My Aunt, Dying

My mother heated her some soup today,
chicken noodle, the first food she's wanted
all week, though she drinks water and Gatorade
often enough, the cancer is making her stomach large
my mother says she doesn't speak much now
and when she does her voice
is small, as if from a place much farther
away than the kitchen table where they sit
on a late August afternoon in the year 2006, two sisters,
the older watching the younger leave, day
by gradual day as if, in kindness, offering the big sister
the chance to take it in, sip
by gentle sip.

Shaking

Kathleen Grieger

I try explaining
to the neurologist
how the seizures
affect my children

Swinging his arm
in my face,
he responds

"What, the kids
are afraid
to see Mommy's
arm shaking?"

Surprised
by the motion
directed at me,
I am shaken

Smilo at Night

Gary Weinstein
Dearing Writing Award, Honorable Mention
Faculty/Employee Division

The playground swing screeches rhythmically, penetrating his fractured sleep. Neighborhood noise percolates into his half dreaming, then dribbles away. One moment the room is dark enough; the next, infuriatingly bright. Smilo Hawkins rolls over again. He cracks an eye to glance at the clock, then checks himself, "It's probably only 2:30 p.m. Forget the time. . .I'm dreaming. Strange loose notions. Go mad! NO. . .just sleep!. . . relax. . .stop thinking," he thinks.

After three years working the day shift at Walker State Hospital, Smilo Hawkins' fourth spring was breaking over the earth, and he'd stopped worrying about seniority. He was clean and focused, and he was working. Shit, he'd been off parole now over a year and things were *good*. And he hadn't known good.

Just Sunday he'd phoned his mother and reveled in it. She'd said, "Oh Miles, I'm so happy for you, son. Steady day work is a blessing and good for the soul, you know, and I'm glad it makes you happy. Your daddy would've been so proud the way you've come around. And working his halls like you are. My oh my, Son!"

They still talked about Smilo's dad, Tyrone Hawkins, at the hospital; the "Forty Year Man" who opened the place somewhere back there in the 1950's. He was given a gold-plated set of keys when he retired. Smilo knew those keys, gathering dust on his daddy's dresser.

And he could hear her tears in how she spoke. "If only he were here to see you now, Son." But Ty had died suddenly of heart failure back while Smilo was in prison, a source of pain for the family never far from anyone's consciousness. Talking with his mom tonight though, feeling grown up, thinking of his daddy, things for once were good. He now knew every inch of the hospital; what lay behind every door, where every tool could be found, how warm the wiring could be allowed to get, which jangly key ring served which emergency. He sometimes wondered if his father had handled the very key rings he now carried.

The boilers, the heating and cooling infrastructure, the chase system linking essential ducts and wire harnesses throughout the whole glorious place, Smilo knew. Some days he felt he alone kept the entire hospital humming. He'd even become someone who said the word *infrastructure* and knew what the hell he was talking about.

Doctors in scrubs, women and men in suits, all said hi to Smilo Hawkins. He was known. He was trusted. They acknowledged him by name and nodded. He often thought, "If they only knew." It was three years now, going on four. By summer he'd be looking at Supervisor I. He wasn't even thinking any more about getting high, or about the hood crowd, those fools, or about the runnin' and gunnin' from back in those days. Now, every day punching in, and every payday pulling that envelope put another couple weeks and years between the old Smilo and the new. Moving him closer to his daddy.

Sometimes he wondered if good was too good.

Last Friday, just a week ago, though it already felt like a year, right at punch-out at the end of his week, Rucker had motioned to him, and Smilo could see in his supervisor's watery eyes that something was up. Smilo sensed Rucker's anxiety and the pleading in his face before any words came out of his mouth.

"We've lost all these people, Smilo," Rucker blurted. "We've lost key people. We're down four just since New Year's! You know what I'm saying?"

"Yeah, I know…it's…" Smilo began.

"We're hurtin' and I gotta make a move, Smilo. I have to put you on the One Shift," Rucker said, pouring it out, all at once, his eyes burning and glaring in his own kind of troubled trance.

"The One!? You mean the Overnight?" Smilo said, standing still as the news bled through him.

"I hate this, Smilo! I hate doing this but I'm boxed in. I need a leader for that crew. I have to start you Monday—Monday midnight. Yeah, the Overnight." Rucker continued pushing his own speech. "Three months, the max. There's two new hires: Billy—you've met him—and a really sharp female, Cynthia. They're quick. It should be OK for you, Smilo. Ninety days. I don't see it longer than that. OK, my man?"

Smilo stood lost. He felt ambushed. He hadn't seen this coming; his old fighting, intimidating ways were rusty. He just stood there and took it, not going mad, thinking it best to keep the job, to keep everything he'd earned. But he walked away burning, torn up inside, feeling betrayed by Rucker and by himself for not objecting. Was this shift change to "crew leader" a good thing? Was it for real, like a promotion? Or was Rucker just playing him?

A panicky gloom built around his rage all the way home. "What the *fuck!* How come me? Goddamn it," he shouted, alone in his car, punching the seat. "The overnight?! That's for freaks, man. That ain't me! When am I gonna sleep? What if I don't sleep? I'll lose my freakin' mind!"

Once home, inside his front door, he stood before the closet mirror and saw himself with jarring clarity. Staring into his own eyes he examined the roundness of his face, inherited from his mother; the freckles sprayed high across his cheeks and the contour of his lips that were his daddy's; his caramel skin, the color of flame, the marriage of his mother's and father's tones he often realized he saw in virtually no one else. "He knows I'm mixed. That's why he's doing this." Then he thought again. "No, maybe it's because I *am* good. And this is how he rewards me? Whatever."

He felt angry, and he felt angry about being made to be feel angry. And this, he knew, spelled trouble. This was one thing he'd learned in the rehabs and from the counselors in prison. "People, places and things…stinkin' thinking…triggers." It was all flooding back as he stood before the mirror. But Smilo had no intention of unraveling, even though all at once it looked much nearer than it had in years.

The next morning, Saturday, he played an angry round of golf with Theo and Donny, cousins he'd been close with from childhood. They were family that had stood by him his eighteen months in State on assault charges nine years ago. The springtime course was just drying out. The bare April trees and grey, matted grass matched his mood: barren, beaten down. Smilo, Donnie, and Theo were often the only black faces on the course. They were their own world. They listened to Smilo; they cursed along with him; they gave advice.

"Man, there is not one ounce of defeat in you, Smilo. You hear me? You remember that. You stand tall; you make this work, man. Sometimes you just gotta step up, you know. They're always testing us. You know that." Donny offered.

And from Theo, "Smilo, brother, turn it around. Maybe there's some hidden something in it; some surprise, some good thing unexpected. Who's this new female? Know what I'm saying?"

They had his back, and he was lucky to have them. This was their best take on things, he knew. He carried their words away with him, but still he felt fury and worry.

Monday he returned to the range, but alone, and only to drive balls. He was in no mood for the course by himself. "What am I doing here?" he asked himself peering around at the empty range. "I'm supposed to be at work." The shift change loomed that night. He stormed home irritable and fretful. He had flash memories of the day he was released from State, those first moments outside the fence in civilian sunlight, in street clothes, untethered, nowhere to go.

He reviewed his plan with himself as he forced down some dinner, tensing himself for the coming changes, "I'll set the alarm, sleep 'til eleven, then go in. Weird. . . ." He drew the curtains, tucked them in tight around their sills, and placed a heavy shirt over his eyes. With sheer will he drifted off. It was just before six in the evening in the strange April dusk.

The alarm jarred him awake, disoriented. Major parts of his brain were still shut off as he dragged himself from bed, into his clothes and out the door. He entered the usual building but was greeted by an entirely different shift of indifferent workers without sympathy or recognition. He might as well have been reporting to a new job on day one in some strange city. The hours crawled by in a surreal haze. "I'm working all night. . ." he kept saying to himself, as if to keep oriented.

Billy and Cynthia were cooperative, quick learners. Rucker was right on that. But Smilo felt a smothered contempt beneath everything he told them the entire night. He walked them through the routines, showed them the breaker boxes, the shutoffs, the switches and gauges that made the hospital run. "Ninety days, bullshit," he thought, driving home. "They'll be ready in a week. What's Rucker thinking?"

Back home a new confusion took hold. The sun was coming up and he could not recall what day it was. "Oh yeah, Tuesday. Morning." It was eight o'clock. "And don't forget," one sluggish part of his mind told another, "you go back again tonight." He slumped into his living room recliner to rest, then remembered to go to bed.

His brain felt soupy, with the crush of a headache pushing in from the back of his skull. "Should I go to bed now? Or should I wait? I'm exhausted now. It's fine. But am I tired enough?" Quickly, he sank toward sleep, but a car muffler on the street out front rattled him awake. A moment's quiet let him drift off again as *he ran through halls of blue carts that got in his way and clocks rotating beside his face. Go mad! The stupid rumbling engines of Toby's car filled the helmet of flowers,* until he awoke to the construction generators firing up for the day at the bottom of his street. It was the start of the workday for the majority of the world. "Oh my god," he thought, "I'm sunk." He scrambled for the earplugs he'd purchased at the pharmacy. He wadded the shirt for his eyes that had worked the night before. In the playground across the street the swing screeched rhythmically, penetrating his fractured sleep. *He tossed and tossed in Theo's boat, but a towel blocked his breathing until the crowd at the lake picked him up and yelled his name "Mine! No!" A dull thunderous chant, and* then the mail carrier thudded across his porch. Kids on their way home from school or skipping out with spring fever squealed in laughter on the sidewalk out front. These intrusions punctured his room, his mind, his sleep.

By three in the afternoon he'd slept maybe two good hours. This would not do. "I'll snap. Who sleeps in broad daylight? How am I going to do this? I won't make the week." He felt like a cardboard version of himself. He imagined himself a ranting, lunatic cartoon figure, loose on the street.

At work no one understood. He brought it up, but got uncomprehending looks. Both Billy and Cynthia had worked nights for years, but were afraid, early on in the job, to give Smilo advice or tell him what to do. They needed him to be with it.

"It's the best of all worlds!" said a coffee-stained fellow they called Tube, when Smilo cornered him in his dull yellow custodial uniform. Tube polished floors at night as all the world slept. As it happened, Smilo's locker was just two over from Tube's but in three years they'd never met, until tonight.

"I got my mornings, I got my afternoons, my evenings too! Then I work!" Tube laughed and revealed teeth that mostly explained it.

"When do you sleep?" Smilo asked.

"I don't!" He laughed again with a wheeze of mingled cigarette and coffee fumes.

By four in the morning when Smilo brought the two new staff to the loading docks to meet the laundry trucks from across town and the hospital supply trucks from Ohio and Pennsylvania, he felt dead inside. The cool night air swept up into corners of the dirty dock, rustling litter and evoking a deep mixture of difficult emotions inside him.

"I'm in trouble, Ma," he whispered into the phone when he got home. "Two nights in and I'm already afraid of cracking up. Or going off."

"Miles, you worry me with talk like that. Would it help to sleep here, at home?"

"No, I couldn't. Thanks, Ma. I have to make this work, here, at my place. But I'm already feeling dizzy, kinda undone. My jaw is tight and my eyes are burning. I don't want to blow this."

Sheer exhaustion knocked him out 'til noon, but as suddenly as he'd fallen asleep, he popped back up into semi-sleep all *afternoon, carrying mail past the tremblers, into the surging flocks of birds. A large balloon. Near the bologna store inside the large building where he held his eyeballs in from falling out and from going mad, he* sat at the edge of his bed, head in hands, tallying the annoyances. The mail carrier, the children, the generators, traffic, even the springtime birds...the damned birds, the swing, the wind. Each took their turn, pinpricking him as he sat there, beginning to tremble. "They all. . .have to stop. I have to do something. . .I have to stop the noises. . .for good, if I'm going to sleep."

Friday night—his fifth on the Overnight—was the worst. The shift was deathly, a unreal dream beyond his reach, shrouded from his brain in a haze of apathy, thoughts of suicide and approaching lunacy. The halls stretched beyond his sight in speckled, salt and pepper linoleum. The fluorescence burned his eyes, reflecting off the flooring in gleaming bands as he death marched through his rounds. His body hurt. His head throbbed. His jangling keys were too loud. When Cynthia and Billy spoke with him it was as though through cotton.

The weekend passed in a lost, befuddled mess of despair. He watched TV but took in nothing. He napped in a sweat with his jaw clenched. He called friends but hung up before they answered. He tried to read, but the words just swam.

Monday noon brought new anguish. Week Two, he thought. "I will NOT go mad over this." He lay down, trying for five hours sleep but felt a new twitching in his eyelids. The playground swing. Again. Two loud cars. A pause. The mail carrier.

He threw off the covers and sat bolt upright, electric, enraged, *"Agggh! That's it!"*

He stormed into his basement, giggling now, "I need some things. I WILL END ALL THIS NOISE. I can! I have to! I have to sleep! They have no idea what's coming!! This is me! Here comes the Cracked Smilo! Go mad, go mad. . .Mine! No!!"

He stuffed things into two crumpled plastic shopping bags and burst out the front door.

First, he clipped a note to his mailbox, "Hold mail at Stevenson Station. No delivery 'til further notice."

Then he stormed to the bottom of the hill where the lunch-break generators sat idle. He dragged the construction wooden horses into the road to block all traffic. With a lusty exuberance, proud of his inventiveness, he stuffed one golf ball each into the generators' exhaust pipes and hammered them solidly in place, bulging the pipe ends.

Giggling. . .*Go mad!*

He marched to the top of his street, across from his house, to the playground where children and mothers lounged comfortably, innocently unaware. "They must wonder who the hell *I* am!" he thought to himself. "It's all over now."

The screeching swing.

He fished through his bag. Moms whisked their children up into their arms and scurried away fearfully while he climbed all over the swing set, spraying aerosol lubricant in every direction, at every moving part.

Next he cut the three bird feeders from their wire lines in his neighbors' yards and plunked them courteously on their respective porches. *The end of birds.*

He victoriously re-entered his house. He stripped off his clothes, felt his nakedness, and collapsed back into bed. He laid still, his hammering heart slowly easing, though still resounding in his ears. He listened.

No traffic. . .No squealing song of the swing. . .No birds. . .No mail carrier. . . No construction. . .just good, lasting, quiet. And no harm to anyone. . .ah. . .here comes a little sleepiness. . .*yes. . .so quiet now the swimmers could move out from the beach. My key ring, like a raft, big and silent. . .long halls for the water. There's Billy and Cynthia and Rucker with their funny shorts on. . .they have the boat, held above their heads. . .and the waves now, so smooth, the water in the bologna store. . . .*

Wednesday Night

Melissa Cloonan

It's five o'clock on Wednesday night. It's shut down time.

Dinner? Check. Changed? Check. ID? Check. Bug spray? Check. Keys? Check. Drugs?

Check.

Great—load the car without acquiring anymore bruises on your legs or sweat down your back, you just changed your shirt so try to keep it dry before you get to clinic. But it's ninety plus degrees and humid—

Just be thankful you weren't out hunched over in the scorching hot fields all day picking strawberries and blueberries just so all of suburbia can have their decadent summer fruit.

So suck it up, load the car with the three thirty-pound boxes of cure, and get to Jefferson.

It's six o'clock on Wednesday night. Who's here and who's still coming?

The coordinators here? All five? Yes. Check. All MSII's here? Check. Translators?

Check. Residents? Check. Faculty? Check.

Pick a car and let's roll. It's so hot and humid and my stupid car has no A/C and I only think I know where I'm going with a car full of people I know from school or clinic or whatever—

Just be thankful they all speak your language and you can have conversations without confusion and communicate exactly what you mean to say and that you are at least traveling in your own country even if you don't know where you are going you at least know where you are which eliminates any apprehension you might have about the situation and if you did have questions about anything you wouldn't be afraid to ask for directions because this is home and not some big foreign country that might not want you here.

It's 6:40 on Wednesday night. It's setup time.

Tents? Check. Lights? Check. Tables? Check. Supplies? Check. Files? Check.

Drugs? Check. Water? MINE, I mean, Check.

Is everyone here? Yes—well don't just stand there, get moving and pitch a tent or something…hurry up, group meeting in five and then we start—MOVE.

Just be thankful you're the one setting up and not the one waiting to be seen because you think you have that thing you know that scary virus uh HIV is it? Because you have this rash on your arm and you don't know what it is or where it came from but your friends tell you it's probably HIV and that you should get it checked and you know you've been having unprotected sex but is that really what it is it's just a small rash it's not like that other guy with the spots all over him maybe he has HIV too if anyone had it, it would be him because look at him he looks worse than you.

It's seven o'clock on Wednesday night. It's show time.

In-take ready? Check. Care teams ready? Check. Pharmacy ready? Check. Out-take ready? Check.

Let 'em in, folks. Ahhh, finally a reprieve for me. My pharmacy is set to go, but it will be awhile before I receive my first prescription to fill, which means I can hang out, dry some sweat, and drink some water during my calm before the pharmaceutical storm.

Just be thankful this little time-out is to wait for scrips from patients and not to wait to be seen by the care teams because you think you might have HIV because of this rash thing and while you wait it's with some white stranger walking you through all those white forms and then asking you a bunch of questions you don't always understand and hope you that you give the right answers while they squeeze your arm and pinch your wrist to get some numbers that they tell you are *bien* and you just smile because they seem really nice even though you don't know what the numbers mean and then you wait to go into a tent.

The eye of my hurricane continues as my eyes capture every moment around me. I feel like I am in my own calm with everyone hurriedly scurrying around, trafficking patients, filling out paperwork, making supply runs, take vitals, and simply sweating. Everyone is quitting their nightlife to continue their day job in the name of humanity. I savor this moment of calming chaos because I know the selflessness of medicine will not always be as evident, if present at all, in the hospital on rotations or during residency . . . .(Pharmacy, you have a call in Tent Five, please. Pharmacy, call in Tent Five. Thank you.). . .

It's 8:15 on Wednesday night. It's fix-lick-and-stick time.

Boxes open? Check. Pill counter? Check. Vials? Check. Labels? Check.

Ok, where's the scrip? Wait, there's no quantity, how many do you want? I know we have it here somewhere, I'm trying to find it. You want ninety tabs?

(Good thing I count fast). No, I don't need help (I've been busier). No, I really don't need help (I work retail, this doesn't even compare). Ok, fine I'll take help (because then people will leave and everyone is happy). I know, I told them I didn't need help. Yes, we have Bactrim DS. No, we don't have Flagyl, but we can get it (great, I hope he can live without *cerveza* for a week). Yes, I can give it to David like last time. No, I don't have condoms, I gave our stash to the nurses at out-take. If we fill it at the hospital, I need the scrip on an official blank. We don't have enough ibuprofen 800 mg, 600 mg ok? No, condoms are at out-take. Interpreter please! NO, I DON'T HAVE THE CONDOMS (what kind of farm is this?). Thursday at 2:30 is fine. (I hope I'm not the last one out again). You hope you're not the last one out again?

Just be thankful you get to leave at all you could be one of the patients and have to live here and work here and you're worried about being the last one out? Maybe you should worry more about what you're doing like dispensing medications to people who need them people who can't sleep at night because their back pain is killing them from being hunched over all summer or their indigestion is keeping them up or the thought of having HIV is worrying them and they can't sleep maybe you have these nasty bumps covering your entire body and you don't know what they are and the medicine you need they don't have and who knows when you'll get it and you would have liked to have seen someone sooner but you didn't want to be sent back to Mexico because you need this job to send money home to your *hijos* and if that happens you may never be able to come back here to work. . . .

It's ten o'clock on Wednesday night. It's closing time.

Everyone have their scrips? Check. Everyone been counseled? Check. Everyone sign? Check.

This is the last scrip, I just need to finish the label and have him sign for it. No, don't take the tent down yet, I'm almost done. Ok, I guess you can take the tent down (it was keeping the bugs out, but if you must). No, the boxes can't go yet, I still need to put stuff in them. Ok, where did he go, he needs to sign. *Firma aqui, por favor. Gracias.* Yes, that can go. I think that's it, my car is loaded thanks to my helpful colleagues and all of my passengers are gathered and ready to go. Let's roll, but let's pick the right on-ramp this time—690 SOUTH. On the road again—

Just be thankful it's the road to home and not the next farm and that it's the road south to Syracuse and not the road to the South for the next round of growing season although as long as you keep migrating around the farms in *Los Estados Unidos* at least you know you're making money to send home and then it's not so bad as long as you don't get deported even though you do miss home and wish that you could be there with your family.

It's eleven o'clock on Wednesday night. It's bedtime.

Shower ready? CHECK!

Everyone is home safely and I successfully unload the three thirty-pound boxes of cure, although I won't know if I acquired any bruises until morning. I'm soaked in sweat and bug spray and desperately require a shower before retiring for the evening. Tonight was a success as our care teams carefully diagnosed and I quickly prepared the necessary cures to our patients tonight. Tonight was a success, but what about tomorrow night? Or the night after that? I think we return to that farm in a few weeks, but what about in the meantime? Or after the clinic is over? Then what happens?

Just be thankful that tonight happened at all and that it was a smooth success because any healthcare is better than no healthcare when you don't feel as though you have access to healthcare or that anyone cares about you at all because usually all anyone ever cares about is how much you harvest and how long you work and sometimes it's just seeing smiling faces of people that are just trying to be nice and who will listen to you and your complaints even though you aren't one to complain that just makes you feel better—

be thankful for
Wednesday night.

Barbara Nevaldine ~ *Grand Tetons*

He Remembers Listening to Canaries

Marilyn R. Mumford

Now at last I know what eunuchs felt—
the loss, the loss—
not ordinary slow repeal of memory,
but swift and brutal slicing off
of all that went before.

Dull knife hacking at body parts,
loud rasp separating song and bone
I see at last
all sexuality parted from what is lost
to time, the surgeon's saw.

Sing, little castrati!
Sing, little canaries
out in front of
or behind your bars!

Rock back and forth
the wooden perches
of your remembering—
Give true vibrato
to your tiny-throated songs!

Diagnosis

Elisabeth Farrell

After checking the stove over and over
to see what I'd seen and didn't believe—
burners off and cold—it occurred to me,

there must have been a portent in my past—

a forecast of this daily ritual, this circle
round and round the kitchen, flipping switches,
trying to contain a fire already raging.

Cual es el internet?

William Hahn

Coffee.

I was walking through a dusty little volcanic valley-town, populated by those wretched *campesinos* who worked the *cafetal* (coffee-land) folded into its rolling deep green hills. On a clear day, from a high-point, you could see the Pacific, but the ocean seemed very far away indeed, and the local market was devoid of fish. The wider economy revolves around the cultivation of coffee destined for foreign markets, primarily the high-end, full roast "latte-sipping" crowd interested in buying "fair trade" of the finicky Arabica variety, dependent on the microclimates of the steep volcanic hills for its unique, chocolate-hinted flavor. The *hombres de café* drank bitter the robusta variety, marketed as Nescafé, grown mainly in the flatlands of Brazil, made sickly-sweet with cheap cane sugar grown by their still more-wretched cousins to the East.

In pre-colonial times, the area—then called Soconusco—marked the furthest reaches of a mad, blood-thirsty Aztec war machine driven by a heady brew of religious fervor and economic exploitation that had marched out of the floating lake city Tenochtitlan in the Valley of Mexico to conquer what was then the "Chocolate Coast" and everything else in the intervening countryside, all without wheels. When the Spanish *conquistadors* came, with their cannon and microbial allies, they parted the Aztec wave like the proverbial Moses, and the area was the province of no empire until a mad *caudillo* in the capital enticed a new wave of German adventurers with land grants and the romantic promises of exploration of the unknown around the turn of the last century. Of course, these hardy wander lusters couldn't do it all by themselves, so the central government press-ganged a captive labor force from the indigenous Mayan highlands. The descendants of these work crews had lost their language, dress, and culture. Now they cultivated coffee, a crop originally smuggled out of Indonesia through a series of diplomatic intrigues involving the seduction of the Dutch ambassador's wife.

Finca is an interesting word. The matriarch of the particular finca I stayed at, a blue-eyed, steely-haired German-Guatemalan-American—a marvelous hostess—who seamlessly transitioned from Spanish to English, used *farm* as the English equivalent. This elides much of its intended meaning, as *finca* certainly has elements of feudalism that are lost in translation. Like any modern farm, however, a finca's intended purpose is to turn land into cash via intensive cultivation of green crops (coffee), a more difficult proposition than one might suspect. In this blood-drenched valley, after surviving a brutal civil war fought as a proxy battle between two superpowers, these businesses were failing because, as one observer in London who had made a killing speculating on a continual lowering of prices noted, "coffee may be black and liquid, but it is not oil." In the modern world, there is always a population more wretched, and now these fincas, like the factories of my rust-belt hometown, are failing due to an inability to compete on a global scale. Ironically, in both places the cost of labor had become too expensive; the laborers scoffed at the Vietnamese who were driving them out of business. "Seventy-five cents a day… who would work for that?" Their daily salary was less than five dollars.

The Tailor.

My current guide Oswaldo was a tailor by training, but he had recently been driven into the roadside stand (read: bone-crushing poverty) business by the "Paca" men, entrepreneurs who had gotten contracts from various international aid organizations to sell second or third-hand American clothes, usually donated to charitable organizations like the Salvation Army. Old men in the town now proudly displayed on their chests such American cultural ephemera as early '90's black hip-hop groups like NWA and Biggie Smalls, advertising slogans such as the Budweiser frogs, and other stomach-punching oddities such as Gore 2000 campaign shirts, all cleanly sheared of any meaning or significance. Obviously, there was now no need for a tailor, as, like manna from heaven, the town was suitably attired in cast-offs from its charitable neighbor from the north, significantly cheaper than the hand-sewn products my friend had previously used to feed himself.

Oswaldo was functionally illiterate, but knew enough to keep a ledger of the sales of his roadside stand, mocked by the local distribution man from the perch of his pickup truck. I had purchased his friendship by buying an orange Crush soda every day. Bored, in hope of some gainful employment, he had agreed to shepherd me around town in my work examining the opinions of the locals regarding their health care system (predictable conclusion: dismal). I don't think he ate as often as he would have liked.

During one of our last conversations, after we had witnessed the surreal scene of a government health apparatchik assuring us that he would treat all comers, regardless of their possession of a government card, because it was the "right thing to do," as his assistant hustled a bleeding man out the back of his office because there was no "medicine" there, Oswaldo asked me, "What is this internet? I keep hearing about it on the evangelical radio."

The Guatemalans have a great expression, *saber*; when taken literally it means "to know," but the more colloquial translation is "who the fuck knows?" I didn't know how to explain the internet to an illiterate man who had never used a computer, so I just said, "*Saber.*"

The Word.

As I walked through town one day, a man approached me, politely asking me to sponsor his evangelical church's speakers so he could spread the Word. Although I had no money for such an endeavor, it briefly passed my mind that it would be somewhat ironic, as a strict non-believer, to be responsible for the daily waking of the valley that a first-world investment in the technology of loud could create. After a couple of minutes' conversation where we exchanged pleasantries and I made it clear that, despite appearances to the contrary, all white people aren't ATMs and my current net worth was probably significantly less than his own (loans and such), he invited me to his church that evening for services. I quickly agreed, despite never having gone to church in any form at any time.

Later, as I entered the cement-block, cement-floored building, *Nueva Esperanza* (New Hope) painted above its door, the itinerant preacher who had asked me to sponsor his speakers was standing at the back, with outstretched arms, next to a cheap, unadorned podium, like something you might find at a high school inventory sell-off. I started to hear his old-time Spanish (everything *vosotros*) ringing six-and-sevenfold off the cheap tin roof. His congregation was swaying, clapping, roiling, rising out of their plastic lawn chairs, "pews," as he called them. He shook his tattered, leather-covered Bible in his left hand, and splayed his arms in a cross, commanding the ancient iconography of his people that predated *Jesuchristo*, etched in stone tablets now buried in the verdant jungle, an iconographic system only the white archaeologists now can comprehend, unconsciously commandeering the ancient *axis mundi*, a pre-Columbus, pre-Christian ceiba tree, a cross of intersecting ley lines that permit the vision-quester to travel through both time and space, his tone demanding, all reverberations, no clarity:

"And here is this young doctor who—Praise be to God!—is going to bring us the medicine to cure us."

Wild cheering, dancing, rejoicing. The congregation, with their hepatitis-scorched livers, brown bellies swollen with babes or ascites, feet splayed from a lifetime of shoeless walks, infected genital tracts, prolapsed uteri, diarrheic with protruding hernias, tubercular lungs rattling, rasping, the ghost of the SIDA (AIDS) silently stalking their midst, suffering from parasitic diseases, *you do not know*, waved their gnarled, tendonless hands—inevitable consequence of a machete culture—and lifted their icteric sclera upwards, giving thanks for this unexpected bounty: a bona fide redeemer in their midst. At that moment, I felt homesick for the first time in my life.

"¿Cual es el internet?"

"Saber."

Last Words

Benita Rogers

I walk down corridors
of bodies gone awry
to that solitary door
at the end of the hall
where my father lies—
a bundle of medical diagnoses
defying all odds
that life could persist
amid such assaults

yet what comes forth
from what remains
is never a complaint
nor railings against the gods
but the few words worth the effort
are simply, all of love

as he lies there on and on
pared down daily
by disease
refined, but not defined
by pain
he conveys one message
and one message only—

all, all,
is distilled
to love.

The Hat

Chris Anne Strickling

I bought a hat last week at the Mercado Benito Juarez here in Oaxaca for 250 pesos, the equivalent of two dollars and fifty cents. I'd resisted buying one in the States because they were all expensive and sported either an extravagant bow or a spray of fake flowers—a silly kind of young girl-ness that put me off. I'm fifty-three. But this hat, it's everyone's Mexican hat. If I put it on right, the wide brim of flexible, almost-white straw flops down just when the sun reaches my eyes. A narrow woven scarf drapes into a loose knot at the back, never sure whether it's a hatband or a bow, adding a flash of color and a hint of things feminine at the back. It looks good on me.

My friend Joyce wore a straw hat, though it was not nearly as exuberant as mine. The straw was darker and there was more hat than brim, more like a working class man's bowler or a derby than a lady's hat. It was never intended to be a fashion accessory; for her it was pure function. A raggedy affair worn on days when she ventured out into the Texas sun in the afternoon, to shield her from the heat and protect her skin. On those days, she'd load up her purse with the spare change and chewing gum, checking to see that she had the electronic door opener for her front door, then strap the cell phone into its case on the arm rest of her power wheelchair, lock the windows, turn the air conditioner down to save money, and shoot herself down the ramped entrance at her front door, out into the world at top speed (which was approximately eight miles per hour). The hat did its job, working collaboratively with lavish portions of SPF 40 sunscreen and a decidedly durable coat of mosquito repellent. She couldn't move fast enough to deter a mosquito any other way. Cerebral palsy is like that sometimes. With these precautionary measures, even though she was always out in the sun, raising whatever hell she had planned, her porcelain skin maintained its beauty and reliable luminosity. She counted on her skin to be pretty, no matter what.

She relied mostly on herself, for everything. At forty-seven, living alone in her own home as a woman with significant physical disability, she had arranged her life to accommodate her marked and different body. Able-bodied visitors to her house in Austin, Texas, had no place to sit because she had removed all of the furniture to make way for her wheelchair. All of the table surfaces were at just the right height for her use; the microwave sat on top of an adjustable height computer table. Interior doors were off their hinges, resting in the garage for a time when someone else might need them. She had no time for negotiating extra obstacles, no need for that kind of foolish privacy. Joyce had business to do. Always. She rode the city bus nearly every day, proudly. Back in the late '80's, she was one of a handful of noisy, sometimes rude disabled activists who pushed the city into making it possible for people like her, whose lives were negotiated from the seated position, to ride the bus. She'd put herself out in the street, right in front of the bus, stopping traffic with her body to make her point. Nobody could stop her, nobody even tried.

She stored her hat in the mesh bag that hung from the push handles of her wheelchair, which was odd because she couldn't reach it on her own. On any given day the hat would swing there in the bag accompanied by a paperback novel with tattered corners, a brown envelope full of bills and hand-written notes, and a Coke. Always a Coke. Like Blanche Dubois, she relied on the kindness of strangers to retrieve the hat from the bag whenever she needed it or put it back when the fierce light of the day had passed. The bag, stretched over those handles, became a tight, narrow space, and the hat was constantly being smashed. But it never mattered, the jostling and pressing made it more pliable, easier for her to use.

One summer morning, just last year, she put her hat on as usual and set out for a visit to the Advocacy, Incorporated offices. Advocacy was something of a home base for her, a place of refuge. She'd been on the Board of Directors there, everyone knew her, and whenever she was in the offices there was no need to explain herself, or to feel ashamed that her speech was difficult to understand, or wonder if she'd be able to get up the ramp or through the door. She trusted that people there could comprehend the fact that, despite what she often jokingly referred to as her "so very horribly disabled body," she was an intelligent, witty, powerful woman. On that particular day at the Advocacy, Incorporated offices she was thinking about her will, feeling her physical vulnerability after a recent and serious illness that had brought her near to death. She told me after that hospitalization, "I don't want to die from something as stupid as a bladder infection. I want to die of something more exotic." She was on her way to talk to her lawyer about designating a new medical power of attorney and to drop in on a friend there. She'd been up late for four days running, calling her long-time friend Lynne in the middle of the night to tell her that a John Travolta movie held a secret meaning for her. There was just enough sense in her story that it wasn't quite clear whether or not Joyce was quite clear. She wasn't able to tell any of us the name of the movie, and I've often wondered which movie she was talking about. Was it *Pulp Fiction*, or *Face/Off*, or *Michael*? Maybe *Phenomenon*, or *Saturday Night Fever*? And what, exactly, had the message been?

On that day, Joyce was consumed with the idea that what she had experienced as support from Advocacy, Inc. for so many years was actually a conspiracy to keep "gimps," people like her, in their place. She imagined that this very public agency made use of a kind of secret password, like some kind of pin number that categorized clients according to their level of need and discriminated against those whose needs were greatest. She was driven to expose the mystery of that code and believed that she might, at any moment, be able to open the doors to some new opportunities for herself if she could just get those numbers right. Patterns of numbers and letters danced in her mind's eye as she drove through whatever barriers there had been between her life of fantasy and the real challenges she faced, to deliver the message, to tell them all triumphantly that she had cracked the AI code. And the code, through some incomprehensible web of connection that only she could make, seemed connected to her hat. She found her attorney in his office, someone she had trusted and enjoyed for years, and told him that she would not be able to talk with him unless he wore the hat. It seemed clear that to wear the hat was to be in solidarity with her. So, he placed it gingerly on top of his slightly balding head, though it compromised his sense of professional credibility and made him uncomfortably conscious of how his hair would look when he took it off. He wore it briefly, just long enough to keep her there before the ambulance came to get her, because everyone—except Joyce—could see that she'd crossed over to a place where we could not go. We didn't find out for weeks that what brought her down was viral encephalitis, delivered by an indiscriminate mosquito.

She lives in a nursing home now because she can no longer manage her own care at home and because there are still not enough resources to care for her there, though God knows we tried everything. But perhaps it barely matters, because these days she only occasionally inhabits her physical space. She lives in a place where words sometimes form themselves and come burrowing up from the quiet of undisturbed ground, at the call of a private sun. And where sometimes they don't. Where pain is a kind of distant throb, and will is a memory just beyond the reach. Where people who love her appear at her side, materially or as part of a fevered imagination, and she is comforted. Where the day plods on without shape and sometimes the drama of the day just gets by her. A place where the blinds are always drawn, but she can still peek through them. The place where sleep and memory are not different, rather parts of a selected experience of daily events. The place where the body receives, takes in, releases, lets go of all manner of nutrients, stimulants, pain killers, mood alterers without so much as a light going on, or off, in the brain to let her know what happened. The place where her good friend Chris visits, and in doing so, becomes Mommy or sister Carol and then Mommy again. A place from which, on some days, it is hard to find "Chris" and harder still to find herself.

The hat traveled with her that day last summer when things stopped making sense, went with her during the months at the hospital, and made the journey to the nursing home. I retrieved it from the mesh bag on the wheelchair one day after I washed her hair; it felt a little like separating old friends. I returned it to her house because I understood its significance. Or at least I thought I did. In October of that year, I went to her house to pick up some papers that needed to be delivered to her lawyer, who had become our lawyer by that time. We'd already been to court to establish my role as her guardian. Joyce's life and mine had begun to overlap in almost every way. As I walked into her empty house, I saw her hat sitting on top of the stereo. I could not move. My chest hurt. No, not hurt. It was a pressure there in my body, like someone leaning heavily. The potent and poignant absence of a longed-for presence. The moment when emptiness is no longer empty, but full of loss. Maybe it was me who was leaning, as I stood inside the small, private space that she so carefully set up for herself. I had to sit down. Sit on the new, but already damaged, floor—because her life in that power wheelchair was hell on floors—and take it in. Just let my face go white and my hands fall down to the floor. Let myself enter into the rhythm of breathing there and try to eat up the grief that was offered to me. Partake of a communion meal in which I received not the body of, not a promise of, but the absence of this woman for whom I had grown to have such feeling. Sat. Still. Breathing. And when I left to go, I must have borne that energy in my body, because when the lawyer saw me there in his office doorway, not more than half an hour later, he knew. He must have recognized the sadness in my shoulders, the traces of intensity still on my face, noticed the worry in my hand, or perhaps he heard the changed cadence of my step as I made my way down that endless hallway to his door. He registered it all in an instant, and said, "Well, maybe it's not a good day to do that accounting stuff. Are you OK?"

I left for Mexico not long afterwards. It was time for a break from the intensity of caregiving. Time to consider what happens next. It would be fair to say that I ran away, like so many others did. I'd watched people, all year long, decide not to care for Joyce anymore, at least in any way she could feel. Disabled friends with long, shared histories of activism, scared off by the intensity of her incapacitation and fears about their own morbidity. Able-bodied friends frightened by her level of need. Old lovers weary from the sadness of such profound disconnection. All of us disheartened to see her bold spirit subdued by illness, to find her will so tentative. And then me, worn out from a year of fierce devotion to a dream of recovery that could not come true. Yet. On my last day in the States, as I left her house, I put her hat on her desk, where she and I had been writing together every Wednesday afternoon for two years. We wrote stories about events in her life, opinions, humorous moments, old songs remembered from "crippled children's camp." On one of those writing afternoons, right before she got sick, she said to me, "I don't go out in the world enough anymore. It's too hard. My stories are going to have to do that for me." She gave me that mission.

I wanted to take the hat with me, wanted to roll it in my hands like some kind of private rosary for the next few months. I wanted to have it for myself. But I left it there as a promise to return to her, to our work, and as an emblem of my hope that before too long she can return to her days out in the Texas sun, with that small, weathered hat to keep her company.

Reneé Mezza ~ *Progeny*

Reneé Mezza ~ *The Rookie*

Kathleen Gunton ~ *Plummeria Cluster*

The Rose

Robert Nazarene

"If love could have saved you
you would have lived forever..."
—grave marker, Elsah, Illinois

The back of my neck rests on the ledge of my tub,
the tub leans back against the edge of the wall
& the wall runs the height of my room to the rafters,

& the rafters lead up to the roof of my home.
The rooftop reaches up through the limbs
& the branches of the tree which shadows me

from harm. The tree gazes out to the steeple in the village,
the steeple climbs skyward to the heavens above,
up over the bluffs which rise beside the river

& the eagles that nest there through the storms—
The heavens look down upon the village below,
& the forests of everlasting arms, & the arms

reach down to the roof of my cabin, & the roof is connected
to the rafters & the attic, above the walls
which climb down to the room where I lay—

& the room looks in on the man in his baptistery,
& the baptistery is turning from warm to cold,
& outside the window is a long-forgotten garden,

& the garden is home to a single red rose, & the rose

looks in through the window into a cold room—
to the man with the back of his neck which is resting,

resting so peacefully against the ledge of the tub—
the man whose last words were: *You,*
are The Rose.

Pamela Ferris-Olson ~ *Pier Geometry*

Abandoned, Abandoner

Whitney Howe

Father, remember how you used to be
With two little girls bouncing on your knee
Remember when the future was yours to hold
And your distant memories were not so cold
But the pain and fear seem to stick with you across the way
And remain frozen in time, even on a summer's day.

The past is what makes us who we are, but does it define us? People think you shouldn't let the past dictate who you become, and to some extent I think that's true. But what about those who are unable to think of anything *except* the past? This is the case with my father. I cannot remember the last conversation I had with him that didn't include talk of warfare or the government trying to wipe out American society. His mind is eternally frozen in his combat days, and hope for his cognitive escape proves more futile with each passing year. The memories I have of my father are few and far between, but the images that I do remember are vivid and engrained in my mind forever. When I remember my father I see episodic images of the past sixteen years that flash before my eyes.

What's In a Name?

Post-traumatic stress disorder (PTSD). I feel like they should rename this type of mental illness. "Stress Disorder" sounds like someone is just overtired. Someone who has no knowledge of this illness could write it off and say, "Get over it. Everyone has stress to deal with." Little do they know the adverse effects it can have on family members, particularly children. My father has been an emotional ghost throughout my life; appearing and disappearing for as long as I can remember.

Although American society prides itself on being accepting of all different kinds of people, when it comes to mental illness it seems as though there is a stigma attached to those who have it. There is a fear of mental illness and a tendency to ostracize those who have it so they will not infect society with their troubles. Those who are unable to "recover" from a certain illness are thought to garner the most sympathy. If the person is able to recover, however, that is when society tends to turn a deaf ear and just wait for the person to pick themselves up again. This hierarchy of illnesses and the stigma can cause those who have the mental illness to not seek help, and family members often feel embarrassed, ashamed or ridden with guilt about their loved one. I am embarrassed and shamed to admit these conflicting feelings within myself, so I can only imagine how many more are out there. When it comes to my father I still don't know if I was unable or just unwilling to cope with his illness.

In War and Peace

My mom always likes to think that my dad went "crazy" after she divorced him. "He was so upset over losing me," she always jokes. My parents' divorce in October 1989 was in fact the trigger for him. He developed the symptoms of PTSD in 1990. I was only four years old when he started to slip away from me. I had come to think that the daily morning Flintstones Vitamins and piggy-back rides would be a constant comfort in my life and would never change. I was wrong.

After my parents' divorce my father stopped visiting my twin sister and me. I don't remember when he moved out exactly. Once I was in a car with my mom and we passed an apartment building. "That's where your dad lives now," she said. That's when it hit me: My dad didn't live with us anymore. He continued to visit our house sporadically, but after a while the visits just stopped altogether and I never knew why. The piggy-back rides disappeared and his demeanor became distant and sullen. At the time I was too young to realize what the word *divorce* actually meant, but I attributed his attitude to the fact that he didn't live with us anymore. About six months after the divorce my mom came up to us and said that our dad was moving far away. He never even said goodbye. It was not until I was a teenager that my mother told me he had been institutionalized at a facility in Maine, and the doctors then declared him as being one hundred percent mentally disabled due to PTSD resulting from his experience in Vietnam and the years of depression that had come along with it.

Wearing Your Heart on Your Sleeve

My father has never been one to care about fashion and most likely has never heard of *GQ Magazine*. His wardrobe consists of faded jeans, a pair of white sneakers, and a million T-shirts. He doesn't give a second thought to the T-shirts he puts on, but those T-shirts are all I think about when I see him. Gray, black, blue, green, the color doesn't matter. The picture, the text, *all* have to do with Vietnam. An ode to Vietnam, a song lyric from Vietnam, a depiction of a battlefield at Vietnam. Sometimes he would spice it up a notch and wear a World War II T-shirt, but the motive remained unchanged. He wanted the outsider to *see* the thoughts that were constantly engrained in his memory in order to express the things he could not say. Every time I saw him he would wear one of those god-damn shirts. The memories of war that consumed his mind slowly made their way to the exterior of his body for the world to see. He became a social recluse. He moved to the woods of Maine to live in solitude, making an occasional appearance on important holidays and birthdays. But even those visits, the ones that were supposed to be happy and joyous, slowly began to fade away. One Christmas my father gave me a book entitled *101*

Ways to Escape a Disaster (the exact title escapes my memory, but you get the idea). While my friends were unwrapping CD's, clothes, and gift certificates from their fathers, I got a book on how to safely escape an earthquake, tornado, or war zone.

As my father's control over his mind's animation seemed to crumble, so did the assurance I had of my own abilities. I considered myself a "normal" person, one that blended in with the crowd but still maintained a unique identity. Every time I saw my father, however, I became scared that I might somehow end up like him. I was scared I would lose control over my mind and my actions. I realize that life is unpredictable and not everything is within our control, but seeing my dad lose his grip on reality heightened my fear. Although I find comfort in the fact that every single person in this world is unique and stands out in his or her own right, I must also take this idea with a grain of salt. There are some types of uniqueness that are socially acceptable and "normal," and then there are those that are not. To be clear, I don't want to completely suppress the very thing that "animates" my father, I just wish he would blend in among the masses a little more.

One day when I was packing up my room to start my freshman year of college, I came across an old photo album. One of the photos was taken when my sister and I were four years old, visiting my grandmother's house in Maine during the summer. My sister and I were sitting on our dad's lap while he read us a children's book. While this photo would seem plain and insignificant to the casual observer, it holds a world of importance for me. My dad is wearing a plain white T-shirt. Just a plain white T-shirt that seems to blend together nicely with my Sesame-Street pajamas. The three of us seemed to fit together, nestled on a faded Lazy-Boy. I put this picture in my desk drawer and pull it out whenever I feel like remembering my forgotten past.

The Over-Identified Child

When I was thirteen years old my mother bought a laptop computer for our house. My sister and I spent every waking moment on this newfound piece of technology in hopes of becoming computer savvy. Shortly after that my father came down for an impromptu visit after visiting his brother. My mother and sister were working so it was just me and him. He saw the computer sitting on the table and asked if I could give him a crash course in computers since he had never used one. I thought this would be an easy way for us to talk to each other until I realized just how much his PTSD had taken over his mind.

All he wanted was to research facts about Agent Orange, to try to uncover the latest government secrets or determine where the next espionage missions would occur. He talked about another world war on the rise and the bastards that occupied positions of authority in the government. He talked of these things with such anger and resentment that tears began to roll down my cheeks. My dad turned his head suddenly and saw me crying, but all he said was, "I know all of this is upsetting. Those government bastards." He then went on a rant about how he would give his life for me in case a war broke out. "Make sure you have enough food and water in storage in case you can't go outside because of all the fighting," he said. I hadn't seen him in over a year and that was all he could say to me.

My mind tried to revert to the power Dorothy had in the movie *The Wizard of Oz*. I wanted to click my heels together and chant, "There's no place like home. There's no place like home." But I was home. This was my life and this was my father sitting next to me. This event triggered distant memories of my dad's sleep abnormalities, attributed to his PTSD. He would call our house at four o'clock in the morning and talk about how terrorists were going to invade America in a matter of months (there is a bit of dramatic irony in that particular rant). After that our phone number was changed, and it was a long while before we communicated via telephone.

It was at that moment I gave up trying to connect to someone who just wasn't there anymore. I just wasn't strong enough to handle his emotional baggage, and the thought of me becoming that way in my adulthood terrified me. It was weeks before I would go near that computer again, but I finally did. Because children who have a parent with PTSD are likely to over-identify with that parent and experience "secondary traumatization," I was afraid that one day I would wake up and become as emotionally distant as my father.

I block out memories of good times with my dad, like when on my sixteenth birthday he gave me my first driving lesson in an empty parking lot. I tend to think of the bad things about my father so as to feel different and avoid those qualities within myself. When I think of my father I think of a man who is a social recluse deep in the woods of Maine who has not worked in sixteen years and prefers to isolate himself instead of engaging in human interaction. This thought terrifies me as I realize that, while this is not a genetic disorder, children of Vietnam veterans with PTSD can exhibit the same emotional problems as the affected parent.

The Struggle of Empathy

There is a great admiration for caregivers who devote themselves to the disabled, whether the patient needs physical or mental care. While others care selflessly for complete strangers as a vocational mission, family members can't always live up to those expectations of care. I view the caregiver as a person who exhibits insurmountable strength and presents a certain stoicism which I have failed to emulate in my own life. For centuries marriage vows have included the adage, "in sickness and in health." At first glance this vow only seems to involve two people; the husband and the wife. It is now seen that the roots of familial relationships spread branches down the family tree and affect future generations. But what if those future generations are not capable of caring for others? What type of stigma does society place on the weak or selfish?

When it comes to my father I can't decide whether I feel nothing at all or a myriad of emotions that I cannot mold into any coherent thought. My whole life I have had to grapple with the judgment I place upon myself for not being able to empathize with my own flesh and blood. It is the truly strong individual who can watch someone's vitality slowly fade away over time. The caregiver makes a vow to be a constant companion to an individual whose diagnosis may never improve. Growing up I've always considered any issue, no matter the topic, to be black or white. There are no shades of gray or "what if" scenarios; there is always a clear-cut answer. When it comes to family responsibilities, however, my opinions get clouded. For example, my father has never given me his telephone number—ever. It has to do in part with him not wanting my mother to have it, but also with his paranoia and lack of trust in other people, which I guess included his own daughters. I always had to wait for his all-too-infrequent phone calls (I never knew when he would call), and then was expected to drop whatever I was doing to talk with him. I never had the option of saying, "Hey Dad, I'm in the middle of something right now. Can I call you back in a little bit?" How long am I expected to indulge his paranoia and suspicions? Will there ever be a point when others will agree that enough is enough, or am I just expected to wait by the phone my entire life simply because he is ill and I am his daughter?

It has been said that the way to develop empathy for people who are ill or disabled is through knowing them. This statement frightens me because I cannot seem to emphasize with my father's condition. Instead, feelings of resentment and restlessness plague my mind. Many veterans diagnosed with PTSD have overcome the disorder and lead "normal" lives. My continual thought process seems to be, "If other people can get better through drug or behavioral therapy, why can't my dad be the same way?" Anger and frustration pulsate through my nerves as I can't seem to accept the fact that my father fits into the thirty percent of combat veterans who go on to develop chronic PTSD and even get worse over time. It is for this reason that I have failed to assume the role of the caregiver. The realization that my father is not everything I expect him to be and the knowledge that he will never be able to connect on a parent-daughter level has forced me to the conclusion that it is better if I stay away, although I am sure that others would have a completely different opinion on the matter.

Tall Tales and Tainted Realities

When I was growing up I had a very close relationship with my grandfather. The epitome of the "classic grandpa," he was never without his over-sized glasses and smoking pipe. My grandfather was a World War II veteran. I remember him telling my twin sister and me stories from his war days. "See this scar, girls?" my grandpa would say as he pointed to his knee. "I got this in Hawaii when I was fighting in the war." My sister and I, sitting Indian-style on the floor, being the perfect little audience for our beloved grandpa, looked up at him in amazement and respect. I couldn't wait for him to tell me new stories; whatever came out of his mouth, I was nothing but fascinated. In retrospect I am sure he exaggerated certain points in order to retain the attention of two seven year olds, but I still have nothing but the highest regard for my grandpa. I miss him dearly, and I would give anything to hear his colorful war stories just one more time.

Remembering my grandpa and reverting back to thoughts of my father, there is a clear dichotomy of emotions I feel for these two people. I think back with loving memories of the one, while I greet my father in person with glazed eyes and barely there expressions. Every time my father opened his mouth I would always want to yell, "You don't know General So-and-So! You have no inside information on government policies!" But I never yelled any of those things. I listened and nodded in my adolescent days, only to begrudge him now in my older years.

My father has stayed the same for as long as I can remember. He always talked about war and government and everything in between. Growing up I indulged his warped rants; I even admit I found them interesting. I had my very own James Bond as a father. After a while, though, a child grows up. They begin to put two and two together and realize some of the things people say just don't add up. That's what happened to me; I grew up. I'm still waiting for my father to.

For those reading this story and telling me to just accept and support my flesh-and-blood, I hope they can also appreciate the difference that exists between these two veterans, my grandfather and my father.

Hasty Judgment

In my personal experience it is the people who have had no experience dealing with someone with a mental illness who seem to be the most critical of how *others* handle the emotional roller-coaster. A month ago my grandmother was in the hospital, and I was forced to be in the waiting room with my estranged aunt and uncle from my mother's side. (At the risk of opening another can of worms, I will just say that my aunt and uncle love to make judgments on situations they know nothing about. My mother has had to bear the brunt of their narrow-mindedness, for which I am deeply sorry). My aunt suddenly brought up the subject of my father and became his personal cheerleader. "You should be patient with your father, it can't be easy for him," she said. I wanted to throw my uncomfortable hospital chair at her head, but I quickly came to my senses (not to mention the fact that the chair was screwed to the floor). "How dare she tell me how to respond to my own father?" I screamed inside my head. She had not seen him since my parents' divorce and had only *heard* of him developing PTSD, yet she was telling me how to deal with it. She sympathized with his situation but was unable to think of how it could affect me in any way. Where the hell was her sympathy for me? Is it only designated for those who actually have the illness? Why should I be patient with someone who has given up trying? I wanted to kick the soap-box she was standing on and make her see *my* reality. I knew it would be of no use, however, since she has never once asked me how I feel about the situation. Words can't express the frustration I feel towards those, especially my aunt, who think a person's disability only affects only the disabled.

My dad refuses to go on any type of medication. He doesn't want to forget his three traumatizing years in the war and believes all therapists want to do is dope him up. I, on the other hand, am quick to advocate for pharmaceutical intervention if it would mean he could emerge from the trenches in his mind. By not taking medication, I feel as though he is enabling his disability, which frustrates me even more. It is this lack of effort that hinders my desire to sympathize with him. He would prefer to lock the door to his cabin in the woods, and I have an increasing inclination to let him.

It is my assumption that people who have a physical or debilitating illness and their family members get a different kind of sympathy and/or empathy from society. It is like first-time babysitters who think watching kids will be a piece of cake because all they do is sleep and eat. Once the child starts screaming his or her head off, however, they have no idea of how to handle the situation. Some vow to return to the child's domain and improve on their nurturing skills while others never go back again. Those who have never experienced such a situation are quick to judge how they would handle it, but once those circumstances present themselves their strength is not all they thought it would be and their judgments change.

What if there had never been any type of war in the world? What would society be like today? Unfortunately that is not the world we live in, and we cannot go back and change the past. One thing is certain, however, and it is that the family structure has been irreversibly affected by the aftermath of violent combat. I used to think that death was the worst part of war because that person can never return. My father did not die when he fought in Vietnam, but I grew up without him nonetheless. His frame of thought is constantly in a combat-zone mentality, because he is unable to shake the trauma he experienced in the past. Now, at twenty-one years of age, I keep asking myself the same questions, "What if my father had never fought in Vietnam? Would he be different than he is today?" The big question is whether or not I can fully believe that it was solely my dad's mental illness that caused him to leave rather than him just not wanting me as a responsibility.

I've come to find that it's the "what if's" that can make you crazy.

Abandoned abandoner,
Please forgive me, for I was too young to fight
I was worried my mind would never see the light
There were too many feelings within myself
And it still haunts me that I could not help

Abandoned abandoner,
I am here today and the sun shines through
I hope one day you can see it too

Onion

Pamela Ferris-Olson

An
onion
at first glance
is an ordinary bulb
layers of translucent
flesh beneath a paper skin
nested together like Ukrainian dolls;
inspection reveals a multifaceted
thing steeped in poignancy.
It's no wonder chefs cry;
with surgical skill
all is exposed.

Intimate details

M. Frost

In his white coat, does he know you,
your sinuses his romping ground?
Your enzyme values fill his hands,
your electrolytes and your blood counts.
Scoping you, he's breathed your air,
seen your septum, touched your skin.
Are you as naked sans your clothes?

Haven't I seen you just as deep,
cradled in my arms, asleep?

Nothing Between Us Now But Love

Rick Kempa

My mother and I are working our way down to Moab, where I will be leaving her in the care of my brother. A road trip with her is a risky thing; in motion, she can become as unmoored as any poor creature in the universe and as desperate. Thus, I have put Bach's *St. Matthew's Passion* in the tape deck, thinking it will soothe her and buy us a hundred or so miles of calm. It's worked. For a long time we have been mostly silent, caught in a spell of organ and strings.

Suddenly she blurts, "What *is* this music? Don't you have anything more lively?"

"Have a look," I say, a bit annoyed that my ploy is failing.

She rummages through the box of tapes on the seat between us and selects the reggae radio mix that my best-lost buddy Bruce taped in Albuquerque in 1980, and that he later willed to me.

"What exactly is reggae?" she asks. "Is it like foxtrot?"

"Well, not exactly, you'll see."

We put the tape in when we pull off the Interstate onto the river road that will eventually take us into town. Bob Marley lets loose an ungodly scream, and I expect her to recoil, but she is perched attentively on her seat. She asks, in fact, which is the volume dial, and turns it up a notch. She guesses at the instruments, tries to puzzle out the words.

At the Dewey Bridge River crossing, I recall, more for myself than for her, how Bruce and I, tripping down this road fifteen years ago, pulled off here and went swimming.

"Naked, I suppose," she says, and I say, simply, "Yes." She asks me then about Bruce—remembers accurately his awkward, lonely aura. She remarks how hard it must have been to lose him.

"Yes, yes it was," I say, surprised that she recalls his passing, that she recalls anything at all about him. And I am moved, suddenly, to be having such a coherent conversation with her, of a sort I had thought I would never have again.

I ask her if she'd mind if I drank a beer to his memory, and she says "No, not at all," so I pull over and get one from the back. She leans back her head and exults in the red rock wonders, the great sheer cliffs, "as if God Himself were playing house." Rounding a bend, we are met with the astonishing white backdrop of the

La Sal Mountains, looming above this red world, and she exclaims, "My lord, I have never seen anything as beautiful as this in all of my born days!"—words that, at home I would dismiss as the quaint hyperbole of a person without a memory, but that out here are the worthy and futile attempts to express an absolute truth.

Now the thoughts are roiling through me: Today, she is not the burden we have let her become in the time that she has been a member of our house, she is not a responsibility that weighs on me, she is not—forgive me—the fretful woman whose continual repetitions I learned to ignore or divert or even, at my worst, rebuke. She is, on this afternoon of wondrous clarity, an old friend sharing a journey on the most beautiful road in the world. I am flooded with a warmth for her of a kind that I do not remember ever feeling, and I think, *Let me pay as close attention to this day as I can, let me imprint it forever.*

Then, as stunning and as chilling as the white flank of that great peak, a contrast of a different sort assails me: For her, there will be no—there *is* no—imprint being made. No chance for us of the rare pleasure that connects two people forever: the shared memory of a day lived well together, a bond as unique as any in the universe. There will be only aloneness, hers and mine, and I feel then a flutter of the unrest that so often rises in her—*this is not acceptable!*

"Mom," I tell her, "it may well be that you will forget this afternoon, but I don't want you to worry because I am going to remember it for both of us."

Her hand reaches over and clasps my sleeve, and her voice rings with relief. "Oh *would* you please? That would mean so much."

"I promise," I say, and it is a long time before she lets go.

We come upon a dirt road forking to the left and I veer onto it, and we advance more slowly into the next dimension, where the earth, the road, the very air is suffused with red. I roll down the window; she edges the music up a bit more. After awhile I say, "Well, you know, it may be some time before I can turn this thing around," and she says, "Well, I'm in no hurry for you to do so."

Eventually, we find a place to pull over, and I help her out of the car and, slowly, to the back bumper where we sit, taking pleasure in the tinkling of water in the tiny creek, inspecting a clot of earth and hay at our feet ("horseshit," I say, and she denies it, and she bends down to pick it up, and we pass it back and forth), thrilling to the red whirlwind that sweeps from right to left in front of us ("*dust devil* is too mean a word," she declares, and so we coin new ones, *angel fire, wind rider*), wondering aloud together why things grow where they do and not where they don't, turning our attention time and again to the horizon-line, where three craggy shapes are etched against that piercing blue. She declares them to be St. Joseph leading two women, Mary and Martha, on a journey. The cathedral spires blazing behind them in the late sun are not mere metaphors; they are the place to which the saints are bound.

I look at her, perched on the bumper beside me, her white hair jutting out beneath the baseball cap, a black vest pulled up around her neck, her eyes gleaming behind those dark glasses. She takes a tiny sip of the beer that I pass to her, licks her lips, passes it back. She extends her arm and with her fingertip traces yet again the contours of that sacred height, and again recites the litany of the saints. I realize that I am as content as I have ever been. Come what may, there is nothing between us now but love, just as it was at the beginning.

Ellen Giraud ~ *Resting Swan*

The Hat

Sarah Kuhlman

Sitting next to the bed in the NICU, Ibana wanted to believe that the infant inside the big plastic box, with all the wires and tubes attached, was not her baby. This was not the infant she had carried, the infant who had moved inside her. Her heartache overwhelmed the pain from her C-section incision, but she dared not say anything. The nurse was explaining all the machines and monitors helping to keep the baby alive as though it was routine, the right and accepted thing to do. But this was not what Ibana wanted. Ibana wanted the baby back inside, to grow, to become a big baby, to be born in another three and a half months, to wear the clothes she had been looking at but had been waiting to buy just because something might go wrong.

And it had. It had gone very wrong. First the back pain, then the contractions. Her doctor had sent her two hours from home to this big hospital and specialists. She had spent a week here on bed rest and medication to control her labor. Although he had visited, her husband, Juan, had to work in order to keep his job at the poultry processing plant. The medicine had made Ibana's head foggy and she didn't remember much of that week. And her premature labor had started again in spite of the medication. Because her baby was in trouble, an emergency C-section had been done before Juan was able to get there. And now, without the small life moving inside her, she felt abandoned.

From her wheelchair she could see only tubes and wires and bedding. A receiving blanket, its pastel bears faded from many washings, was rolled to make a nest in the center of the isolette. From her seat, Ibana could not see the baby inside. She was not sure that she wanted to see her. A machine that sounded like a muffled lawnmower growled at her elbow. Then, two tiny feet appeared over the edge of the blanket roll, pushing upward together, and a minute hand appeared, waving at the end of a stick-like arm. Ibana straightened in her chair and peered into the nest.

There in the middle of all the tubes and wires was a dark head, hardly as big as Ibana's clenched fist. The baby was too skinny, her arms and legs as big around as pencils, her stomach huge, much like pictures Ibana had seen of children starving in Africa. White patches on the baby's chest, connected by wires to the heart monitor, were so big that they overlapped, leaving little skin visible. Tubes were coming out of the place where Ibana thought her belly button should have been. One end of a tube attached to her mouth, and the other led to the noisy machine. A small light shone though a bandage on her foot. Lying on her back with her feet and arms in the air, the baby looked like a stranded turtle.

As Ibana watched, the baby squirmed. Her forehead wrinkled, her mouth opened, and she began to cry. But because of the tube through her windpipe, she had no voice. A nurse approached quickly and reached through the porthole of the isolette to place a calming hand on the little head. The infant relaxed. Tears leaked out of Ibana's eyes and onto her cheeks. She quickly wiped them away with her fingers.

"What color are her eyes?" she asked.

"We don't know yet. Because she is so premature her eyelids are still fused. She will open them within the next few days. But a baby's eye color changes over the first few months and you probably won't know for a while." Then the nurse added, "Does she have a first name yet?"

Ibana did not answer. So the nurse repeated the question. "Have you named your daughter?"

Ibana looked up at the young nurse whose face seemed far away.

"Yes," she whispered. "Her name is Jocelyn. Jocelyn Mariana." And as her eyes returned to the tiny figure in the bed, she wondered how she would hold her daughter with all this equipment attached. She wondered if she would ever hold her.

Three days later, Ibana was released from the hospital. At the suggestion of the social worker, she moved into a hospitality house run by a local charity. It was located two blocks from the hospital, and there was a shuttle bus, so Ibana was able to visit the baby easily, in spite of her recent C-section. She spent long days at the hospital and longer nights at the house. She missed Juan terribly. Until she was hospitalized, they had spent every night of the last seven years together. Both had been eighteen when they married. Almost immediately they had left Mexico to come work in the poultry plants in Arkansas. With the help of classes at one of the neighborhood churches, Ibana had learned English quickly. Their employer had helped them get green cards. Being legal made life less stressful, but it didn't make home and family any closer. Juan had become a line manager, but Ibana had left the poultry plant to work as a cashier in a grocery store. Until Ibana became pregnant, they had both worked, sending money home and saving a bit each month, putting off having a family. They even bought a car, one of the few reliable ones in their community of friends. After several years, they thought if they had children of their own, perhaps they wouldn't miss home so much.

Juan had been able to stay with Ibana for a couple of days while she recuperated from the delivery. But if he didn't work, they had no income, and he had had to return home before Ibana was allowed to leave the hospital. Now, she called him every night with a progress report, but she was not able to forget the look of horror on his face when he had first seen Jocelyn. She did not think he was listening to what she told him about their baby. Their conversations were becoming shorter each night. She knew that he needed to work, but she was angry with him for leaving his new family. Sometimes, though, if she thought about it long enough, she could hardly blame him. Even she was not proud of the family she had given him.

During the first ten days, the baby didn't seem to change much. Ibana had learned not to ask about ventilator settings and how much oxygen the baby required at any particular time. This information only confused and worried her. It changed from one hour to the next, and she found herself worrying about the wrong things. An increase in the amount of oxygen the baby required would bring Ibana to tears of frustration. But then she would find that the real worry, the thing that concerned the doctors, was the infant's inability to digest the small amount of breast milk she was able to provide. She would go back to the hospitality house in despair only to find the next morning that the staff had been able to decrease the oxygen level and feedings were being increased. She struggled to find a way to measure progress. When she asked the nurses how the baby was doing she heard, "She's having a good day." Or, "She's stable, but still critically ill." Sometimes one would say, "She's doing as well as can be expected, for her gestational age."

One morning, Ibana was met at the bedside by a nurse she had not seen before. She had gotten used to the routines of several of the other nurses who usually cared for her daughter. She was tired today and not looking forward to the added stress of things being done differently.

The new nurse smiled and said, "Hi, I'm Alice. I'm taking care of Jocelyn today. Would you like to start by taking her temperature?"

It was a good start. Ibana was used to being allowed to take her daughter's temperature, although there were times when some of the nurses thought the baby too unstable for Ibana to touch.

While Ibana was holding the digital thermometer under the tiny arm, the nurse asked, "When was the last time you got to hold her?"

Surprised, Ibana replied, "I have never held her."

"Oh," said Alice. "I think we can change that."

Ibana stared at her in disbelief. "Isn't she too unstable? There are all the tubes and wires. What if something gets disconnected? Won't she get cold? I don't think I could."

The nurse smiled patiently. "We will watch all those things very closely. We'll get her respiratory therapist to help us get her situated. After we put screens around her bed, you can unbutton your shirt and hold her against your skin. We'll put a warm blanket on top of her, and she will stay nice and toasty. You'll see."

"Oh, I would love to hold her. If you think it's all right. But I don't want anything to happen to her."

"I think she will love it. I wouldn't suggest it if I thought it would harm her. Her doctor agrees."

Thirty minutes later, Ibana sat in a recliner, her daughter's small head lying on her chest, her body cradled between Ibana's breasts. Over her back, from head to foot, Ibana held a receiving blanket, folded into a rectangle that she realized was about the size of the magazines neatly arranged on the coffee table at the hospitality house. She had little awareness of the ventilator tubing taped to her shirt as she felt the flutter of the infant's fingers moving against her bare skin. Ibana breathed slowly and deeply. In a low voice, she began to sing her mother's Spanish lullaby.

"It has been a good day," she said to herself as she sat by her daughter's bedside later that afternoon. It was almost dinnertime and soon the shuttle would be coming to collect Ibana and the other out-of-town parents. Alice would be signing out to the night shift nurses in another hour. Having helped Ibana change Jocelyn's diaper, she was busy arranging the nest of linens in the isolette.

"I must knit her a hat," she said. "We usually have small hats her size, but I couldn't find one to fit her. I'll have to make her one. I like the babies to have hats. They lose a lot of heat through their heads and hats help keep them warm."

Looking at her baby's head, Ibana thought about the floppy yellow sun hat that she had been tempted to buy the day before her pain had started. Jocelyn's whole body would have been hidden beneath that hat. Then she remembered the tiny hats she had seen in the social worker's office. Beautiful outfits that looked like christening gowns, each with its own small bonnet, were made by volunteers to clothe the babies who died.

Suddenly, Ibana saw a different meaning to the events of the day. She burst into tears. "You don't think she is going to live, do you? You are going to make her a hat that fits, and you don't think she'll ever outgrow it because she's going to die. You let me hold her today because you don't think she is going to make it, do you?"

Alice stared at her.

"That's not what I meant at all." She was clearly horrified that Ibana had misunderstood. "I have no reason to think that she won't make it. She's still very small and has a lot ahead of her, but I have faith in her. You held her today because both of you needed for you to hold her. It won't be the last time. If I make her a hat, she'll outgrow it and you'll put it in her baby book."

Alice sat with her arm around Ibana, hugging her tightly while Ibana cried. When Ibana was at last able to control her tears, she said goodnight to her daughter and went to catch the shuttle.

Several days later, as Ibana entered the NICU, she saw Alice taking care of another baby. She had not seen her since the day Alice had been Jocelyn's nurse, and Ibana was embarrassed. Alice caught her eye, smiled and waved, and Ibana felt a bit better. One of Jocelyn's regular nurses was waiting at her bedside when Ibana arrived.

"You're just in time to take her temperature." The nurse seemed quite cheerful today.

Ibana peeked into the isolette.

"What's that on her head?" she asked.

"That's the hat Alice made for her."

Ibana could not believe it, and anger rose inside her. She thought Alice had been listening to her. She thought she had understood. What right did Alice have to give up hope for Ibana's baby? But, obviously, she had. There on Jocelyn's head was a small, pink and white knit hat that fit her perfectly.

Then she saw something else. Her daughter was hugging, with both her arms and legs, something knit out of fuzzy pink yarn with a tassel at one end. "What's that she has her arms and legs around?" Ibana asked gruffly.

"Oh," said the nurse. "That's her other hat. Her big hat. The one Alice knit for her to grow into."

Ibana stared at the fuzzy pink tassel nestled beneath her daughter's chin.

Three months later, Ibana stood in the scrub room outside the NICU. Alice stood next to her, holding Jocelyn in her car seat. On Jocelyn's head was the fuzzy pink hat. Juan had gone to get the car. As the women waited for the outside door to open, a woman dressed in a hospital gown sat in a wheelchair rubbing sanitizing gel on her hands and arms.

"She is so small," the new mother sobbed. "I'm not sure I can look at her."

"You have to," her husband said gently. "She is your daughter. You have to find a way to look at her. You must have faith. You must keep hoping." The woman sobbed even harder.

Apologetically, the man looked at Ibana and Alice. "Our daughter was born very early, you see. She doesn't even weigh two pounds."

Ibana looked down at the woman and said quietly, "It is not so easy. I know. This is my Jocelyn. She was tiny, and I have been where you are today. But, let me make a suggestion."

Smiling, she turned and put her hand on Alice's arm.

"Have Alice make your daughter a hat."

Superstore

Oliver Rice

Here is a decor for miscellaneous desire.
Here is a demography of faces.

Here the elevated have a right,
the vulgar,
the fatuous,
in small appliances, in sporting goods,

in children's books,

in the garden center.

The stimuli,
the mores,
the credulities roam the aisles,

*

where beside the pharmacy window,
inserting his arm
into the mechanical device
for taking anyone's, anyone's blood pressure,
Leonard is prepared to confess everything,

*

where the thought comes to Sue on checkout four,
and comes again,
that she is the wrong person for her life,

*

where Alfred in the office
hears a mantra
in the shuffling of the feet,
the clinking,
the rustling,
the humming of the machines,

*

where Ellen senses innuendos of another chance
in home furnishings, in ladies' apparel,

Luis in hardware
receives intimations of a journey,

Russell in the stockroom receives flashbacks
of things that look the same but are not,

*

where Margaret sits at the snack counter
with a god-shaped absence somewhere
among her secretions.

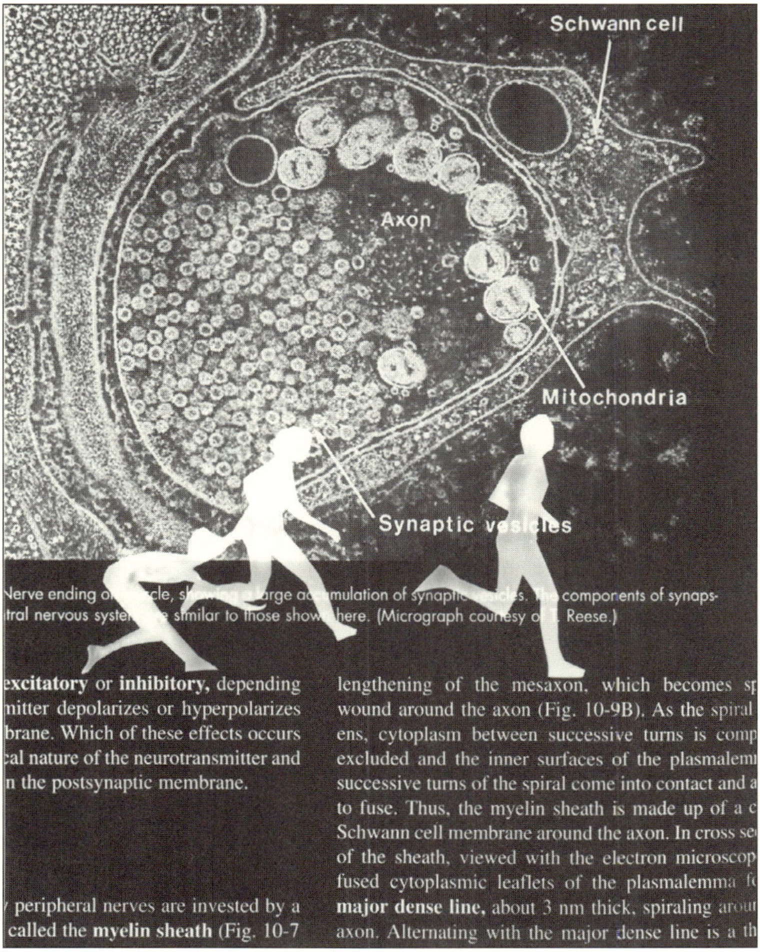

Sarah Nicolai ~ *In Tandem 7*

Right Now

Dotty Holcomb Doherty

Ambushed by regrets,
I cringe, listening to them
mock me.

Deluged by imminent worries,
I wonder where diseases will take
those I love.

I toss, sleepless,
caught in thoughts.

What am I missing?
Right now.

Right now, I lie here nestled in
the fragrance of new spring
captured in these wind-dried sheets.

Right now, your breath
lightly cools my neck;
your arm resting warm along my thigh.

Right now, quiet blankets us;
sweet sleep already cradling you
soft against my back.

Oh stillness—erase my sorrows!
Moon—scatter my worries like dew
for the morning sun to kiss away.

Let me savor, absorb
and breathe
as I rejoice
in you, in us, in now.

Like a Train

Beth H. Evans

Like a train
    rumbling toward a distant bend
    beyond which my vision does not curve
I watch, helpless,
    as you set off
    from the past we held together.

Should I like a remorseful lover
    leap from the platform,
    race behind,
    call you back
    beg you to stay within my sight—

Or do I, like the gored soldier,
    turn from your final moment and
    armed with need
    crawl off to other battles?

A last echoing whistle
from the bend
I see you rounding.

    It is time, it howls;
    let go.

    Let go.

Haunted

Robertina Szolarova

In the slow hours before dawn
the song of the night rises.
I navigate familiar streets
as ghosts drift to meet me

to guide my way forward
to a house where there is another one
who sees ghosts
at the foot of the bed.

I recognize this moment,
this circle of waiting
a room filled
with what is unsaid

where I shall teach
the language of dying
to brother, wife
mother, son

where I will instruct
how many drops of morphine
will smooth
the jagged edges

how to recognize
the shadow of pain
or the light of calm
upon his silent face.

What I cannot translate is
this calligraphy of bones
shimmering
beneath translucent skin.

What I cannot explain is how loss
creeps in gradually
and engulfs you wholly
before you know you're drowning.

I can lead you here
to this very edge
of the known world
and place his hand in yours

but it remains for you to arrange this loss
across your shoulders
and learn to walk
beneath its weight

and I will emerge to find
another ghost guiding my way
hear another voice
join the night-song.

Susannah Loiselle ~ *Sand Fence, Emerald Isle, NC*

Night Duty

Eileen Valinoti

At midnight I reported to Marianne, the evening nurse, to begin my tour of night duty on Female Medical. I felt apprehensive. I was only in my second year of nurses' training, and Female Medical was considered St. Mary's unofficial psychiatric unit. Though most of the patients had heart disease or diabetes or cancer, some were borderline psychotics, dwelling in a never-never land between fantasy and reality. At nineteen, I had little knowledge of psychology or counseling and my own host of fears to confront.

The nurses' station stood at the head of a staircase that led to the male surgical floor below. There I sat, perched uneasily at the edge of my chair, as Marianne gave me the report on the patients, beginning with a Mrs. Greene.

"She's off the wall," Marianne said, rolling her eyes, "and somebody found her smoking the other day. No one knows where she got the cigarettes; she never has any visitors." She paused, and then added ominously, "You'd better watch her. There's an oxygen tank in the room."

I kept my face expressionless.

"A nurse must appear calm at all times," our student handbook read, but in my mind's eye, I could see Mrs. Greene and me being blown to kingdom come. Everyone else was fine, Marianne said, or as fine as they could be under the circumstances.

"Just make sure that no one climbs out of bed. Someone last night wandered onto the fire escape," she added, gathering up her belongings. I had never met Marianne before, but now she seemed the most desirable companion on earth.

"Shouldn't we go over the narcotic count together?" I asked.

"Everything checks," Marianne said, glancing impatiently at her watch. She grabbed her purse and disappeared.

I made my rounds, shining my flashlight into every room, relieved to find that my patients were still breathing. Her first night on duty, my roommate had found a patient dead in her bed and became so unnerved that a senior student had to take over.

"Her hands were so cold," my roommate said, "*icy* cold."

I shivered in the warm hall, thinking about it.

"Hail Mary," I prayed silently, clutching the rosary beads in my pocket.

Mrs. Greene was wide awake, sitting upright in her bed. I saw at once that she was deathly ill. Her skin was dark with jaundice, her abdomen swollen while her arms and legs were as thin as matchsticks. She wore thick dark glasses and had fashioned a piece of black silk into a sort of veil that covered her head. She looked like a mad nun, and, in the dead of night, she was a fearsome apparition.

The room was bare except for a crucifix on the wall. I saw no cigarettes, no photographs or get well cards, no hints of a life before this dreary place. The oxygen tank stood in the corner.

"It's too close in here," Mrs. Greene said in a hoarse voice. I opened the window.

"Now there's a draft." She picked at the bedclothes with long spectral fingers, "Get me another blanket; my feet are freezing."

I covered her legs with a quilt.

"It's too heavy on my legs." As I leaned to remove the quilt, she grabbed my arm.

"Give me something to make me sleep," she said. Her chart read: "NO SEDATIVES."

"I have no orders," I said, looking away uneasily, afraid she would ask me why. I would have to say I didn't know. But she only stared at me, her eyes glittering behind the dark glasses. I felt pity and guilt and revulsion.

A patient's buzzer sounded in the hall. Deliverance.

"Someone is calling for me," I said. Still Mrs. Greene held my arm until I had to pry her fingers away. She sank back exhausted on the pillows, muttering to herself. Her whispers followed me out the door, her murmurs impossible to follow.

At two a.m., Miss Hoey appeared. Catherine Hoey was the night supervisor, an elderly Irishwoman who made her rounds once every shift, inquired briefly about the patients, and offered one coffee from the pot she always carried with her, an evil brew that tore your insides. Miss Hoey was never any practical help, bringing a Celtic fatalism to the care of the sick.

"Sure the day shift will be here soon, love," she would reply placidly when asked for advice.

Once she left, I sat at the nurses' desk and wrote my notes.

"Patient agitated," I wrote, or "Patient confused," the same sad chronicle over and over. The room was hot. Beneath my feet, a radiator hissed and gurgled. Feeling drowsy, I got up to look at the calendar on the wall. I counted all the nights I had to go. Ten, I saw with despair. I opened the window and looked out at the barren view. The hospital stood among a warren of abandoned warehouses. I longed to see a neon sign or some indication of normal human life. Then I heard the sounds of music. Off in the distance, a band was playing. I leaned on my elbow, listening. Out there, not so far away, someone was dancing with someone. I closed my eyes for a moment, lost in a dream of strong arms holding me fast.

I went back to my charts until once more, I was overcome with sleep. I ran to the sink to splash cold water on my face. Time to make my rounds again. And so the hours passed until I heard the clatter of the breakfast trays, the banging of the elevator door, the quick footsteps of the day nurses coming on duty.

In the nurses' residence, I couldn't sleep. I would drift off and then be awakened by the noise of my classmates coming back from the hospital, laughing and slamming doors. When I finally slept, I was haunted by weird dreams in which Mrs. Greene appeared, clutching my hand in a vise-like grip.

The days and nights seemed to blur together. It was winter, and I rose in darkness to go to the hospital and when I returned in the early morning, it was still dark. I began to feel jumpy, distant from the world.

"You look like a hag from hell," my roommate told me disapprovingly one night as I dressed to go on duty. I had given up curling my hair. It hung now in lank, dispirited strands on my collar, in bold defiance of the rules. A strange rash had erupted on my face which I had doctored myself with applications of Vaseline, making it worse.

"Oh shut up," I told my roommate irritably, banging the door as I left. She could talk, I thought bitterly, cozy in her pajamas, a blissful sleep ahead.

One night, as I was writing my nurses' notes, I heard footsteps on the landing, followed by a loud "PST." I looked up, and in the middle of the staircase stood my classmate Terri, who was working nights on the floor below.

"Kelly," she whispered, "I've got cigarettes." She patted her uniform pocket and grinned.

Terri and I were not friends; she was not my idea of a proper nurse. On duty, her cap was often askew, her apron untied. In the nurses' residence, she went about in her brother's old army pants, rolled up to her knees. She chattered and giggled constantly, holding court with other renegade classmates in her shambles of a room. Last week, she had been caught smoking in the hospital cafeteria. I had met her on her way to the Director's office, scarcely recognizable in a navy skirt and a long sleeved white blouse. Her hair, which normally framed her face in an exuberant halo like Orphan Annie in the comic strip, was neatly braided across the top of her head. She looked like the orphan schoolmarm in *Jane Eyre*.

"I want to look young and vulnerable," she told me, eyes downcast.

"I wish you well," I said primly. In my heart, I thought her a silly, feckless girl who deserved whatever she got.

Now she shifted restlessly on the staircase, looking anxiously over her shoulder.

"Come on," she said, pointing to the steps where she stood. "You can hear if anybody calls."

I hesitated. But lack of sleep and isolation had destroyed my willpower. Still, I hung back.

"Hurry up," she said. "Hoey might come back. Sometimes she forgets where she left her damn coffee pot."

Miss Hoey. I was sure that if she ever saw us here smoking, she would drop dead on the spot of a stroke or a heart attack or both.

We sat together on the steps, inhaling deliciously.

"I'm a wreck," Terri puffed happily. A patient had just thrown all his pills at her and told her to go to hell.

"*I'll* get blamed for it in the morning," she said. "Koch hates my guts." Miss Koch was the day supervisor, notorious for her interrogations of the student nurses.

We sat huddled together on the narrow step, our cigarettes glowing. I found myself confiding in Terri, telling her about Mrs. Greene, how frail she was but sinister at the same time.

"Oh, throw some holy water at her," Terri said carelessly.

Why was I even talking to this foolish girl? But I was unable to stop.

"Look at my arm," I said. The skin was mottled and red. "Every time I go near her, she clutches at me."

"What are they doing for her?" She might have been the chief surgeon inquiring about one of his charges.

"Nothing," I said. From one of the rooms, someone moaned softly. "They won't give her anything and she *never* sleeps." I knew now what it was like to be alone and to long for sleep.

Terri eyed me speculatively from behind clouds of smoke.

"You have to use psychology with her. Give her a sugar pill and tell her it's a Nembutal."

Lying to a patient? I might as well consult with Miss Hoey, I thought disgustedly.

A ritual developed. We met every night on the steps as soon as Miss Hoey left. Juan, Terri's orderly, stood watch while I provided the paper cups of water to use as ashtrays. We never sat for long. A buzzer sounded or else we imagined we heard Miss Hoey's heavy tread.

Terri always had stories to tell from her unit—angry outbursts, nervous breakdowns, miraculous recoveries, all ending in the morning confrontations with Miss Koch. Terri told these tales with a theatrical intensity, acting out all the parts, puffing out her skinny chest as the bosomy Koch, shaking her fist as the angry patient. One night a large rat had appeared on the unit.

"Just as I was changing dressings, I saw it scampering across the floor." My hand flew to my mouth, to smother a scream.

"Big as a cat," she said, making a wide arc with her hands to show me its monstrous size. I cringed at the details—the beast's twitching tail, its fierce fanglike teeth, its bristling nostrils. Juan had panicked, crossing himself and cursing hysterically in Spanish at the same time.

"But I looked it straight in the eye and chased it away with a broom." Terri leaned back against the railing, hugging her knees in delight.

I looked over my shoulder. A new terror had been added to the night.

"Don't worry," Terri leaned over and patted my arm, "it's gone now. Besides, you can't show fear," she said, folding her face into stern lines, a soldier back from the wars.

I was speechless with admiration. I knew that if it had happened to me, I would have begged to be relieved. Miss Koch, it appeared, was equally impressed. She looked on Terri as a heroine.

"She calls it 'the animal,'" Terri said, choking with laughter. "Every morning she asks, 'Did you see the animal again, Miss Murphy?'"

We collapsed into gusts of laughter, and we had to bury our faces in our aprons to smother the sound.

* * *

My last night on duty, I was alone. Terri's tour had already ended. A white-robed nun took her place. From my desk, I could hear the soft rustle of her habit as she made rounds, the click of her rosary beads. Cozy chats on the stairs were now out of the question.

I didn't care. After tonight, I would join the real world again—I would go to the movies, dance alone in my room to the radio, eat hamburgers at the diner with my friends. When Miss Hoey made rounds, I gave her a dazzling smile. She looked astonished, accustomed now to my pursed lips and anxious frown.

"Sure to God, love," she murmured wonderingly.

I thought about Mrs. Greene, how she would still be here, long after I was gone, like a prisoner in her cell.

"No one ever comes," the day nurses said every morning, clicking their tongues and shaking their heads. I wished she had a friend to make her laugh and share a pack of cigarettes with her.

I went into the treatment room to get my flashlight. A battered tea kettle sat on the counter, one of Miss Hoey's castoffs. I felt a wave of homesickness. Tea was a ritual in my Irish family, a cup of tea, the cure for every ailment—for headaches, for cramps, for shattered nerves—sometimes even offered for poison ivy and corns.

I put the kettle on to boil. Rummaging in the closet, I found a tea bag. I carried the steaming cup into Mrs. Greene's room. She was awake, the sheet pulled up to her chin, the blankets in a disheveled heap at her feet. It was stuffy in the room. There was a faint odor of disinfectant and the musty smell of the woolen blankets.

What did she think about, I wondered, staring at the walls night after night? I fought back the dread I always felt in her presence.

"I brought you in a cup of tea," I said.

She didn't answer, her expression impenetrable behind the large dark glasses, glasses a movie star might wear to hide from adoring fans. Moving closer to her bed, I heard myself say,

"It's made from special herbs that will help you sleep."

She reached for the cup, but her hands shook so violently, I had to sit on the bed and hold it while she drank. After each sip, she had to rest, spent from the effort. It seemed to me an interminable time while she drank, the only sounds in the room the relentless drip of the broken faucet, the ticking of the clock. I was intensely uncomfortable perched on the bed, a forbidden intimacy.

"A nurse must *never* sit on the patient's bed" had been drilled into us. At last, she finished and sank back exhausted on the pillows.

I was ready to hurry away, when suddenly she raised herself on her hands, reached up and took off her glasses. I saw that her eyes were a startling blue, the skin around them as pale and delicate as paper.

"Turn off the light," she said, blinking and pointing to the fixture on the ceiling. I flipped off the switch, she closed her eyes and once again, fell back on the pillows.

When I looked into Mrs. Greene's room again on the last of my rounds, it was dawn. A streak of pale sunlight fell across her bed. From where I stood in the doorway, I could hear the soft, slow rhythm of her breathing.

Lois Dorschel ~ *Misty Morning*

A Different, Deeper Sort of Calm

Seth Collings Hawkins

Like many people, I assumed the childhood I shared with my sister to be a pretty ordinary one, especially in terms of health. Only two years younger, Katy either endured an ailment with me or, maybe worse, knew exactly what was lying in store for her. We suffered through the standard litany of childhood hardships: chicken pox, strep throat, neighborhood bullies, ear infections, algebra, and so on. The medical treatment we received seems very commonplace as well. By the time we entered junior high school, we had consumed gallons of chicken noodle soup and coke syrup, watched hours of cartoons (only when we were sick), and, more infrequently, visited our pediatrician to be poked, stuck, measured, chided, applauded, medicated, and reminded: "Four glasses of milk a day, Mom, and not those little glasses either—twelve ounces at least!"

Thanks to my mom's nutritional and nursing sense, Dr. Spock, and our pediatrician, we were a model of healthy living throughout grade school. For example, every morning my sister and I enjoyed a bracing dose of cod liver oil; invariably, her share was donated to the bushes outside our house on the way to the school bus. As the bushes never seemed to show any remarkable bloom of health and vitality from this daily treatment, I saw no reason to swallow the stuff either... perhaps my first experience with the scientific method.

But a particularly interesting and—to me—wholly unexpected aspect of growing older is learning how unusual one's childhood really is. I realize now how close my sister came to dying when, as a two-year-old, she aspirated a peanut. My parents brought her to the hospital when she started turning blue, and that began a summer-long battle to remove the entire peanut, a struggle which was never fully successful. The experience was a terrifying one for my parents, and as they shuttled between specialists and nights sleeping on hospital cots, I could feel my first-born hegemony over their attention coming to an end. That's how I package it now. At the time, I just got crabby at all the attention she received. I never truly conceived of the whole incident as a medical situation which my sister and parents *suffered* through until years later. In its coded, compressed form, I filed it under family dynamics and social interactions. Its physical and medical dimensions were secondary and implied. In this way, as a kid, I normalized my own and my family's experiences. It worked so well that I begin this essay by referring to my sister's and my childhood health as "pretty average" when, in fact, she suffered a trauma that required five bronchoscopies at one of the finest medical institutions in the country to prevent her death.

Childhood usually involves frequent and minor transitions between health and injury or illness, and children grow accustomed to such transitions. A key part of aging may be the growing realization that any sickness or injury is a state of real unhealthiness, a dangerous place to be. In my family, my typical sick role was to turn into a saintly child, and why shouldn't I have? I stayed home from school; I got to watch TV, eat what I wanted when I was able, and anyway, none of my symptoms were ever too serious. Being sick was a chance to receive special treatment, at the small cost of running a fever, getting an infection, or (worst of all) throwing up. Any further symptoms were more interesting than scary, like the time I went delusional from a fever and watched fluid black blobs drool across the wall for half a day.

My true calling was never illness. I was a trauma junkie, and even there I encountered nothing that seemed truly dangerous or threatening. I did my best over the next twenty-some years to rival my sister's brush with death experience: flipping off bikes, jumping through plate-glass windows, being stabbed by rusty nails. My dad recently said he thought my signature injury involved chasing a floating disc while playing ultimate Frisbee and, in my absorption, sprinting full speed into a fire hydrant. One minute I was running, then suddenly everything was clouds, sky and grass as I did a flip-and-a-half in the air. The next thing I knew I was lying on my back staring at the sky. The collision caught me in mid-stride, my left leg rising, and a half-second difference in the collision could have easily shattered my patella. As it was, I just bruised my leg, and that resiliency seemed to characterize my childhood adventures with injury. I was the rubber man, one of my best friends said.

My dad wasn't so sure. The day he dropped me off at college as a freshman, we both paused at the massive gate to say goodbye. I wasn't sure what to expect—words of wisdom, maybe a handshake to recognize my incipient adulthood or a hug to recognize my passing childhood. Maybe he would hand me a condom, or pass on timeless words his father said to him. We both looked at each other. "Don't do anything until we get you on the insurance," he said, hugged me, and walked back to his car.

Nor was my seeming invulnerability confined to trauma. My freshman year in high school, I was sidelined from my swim team for a whole season when an ear infection refused to respond to treatment. It puzzled each physician I saw until finally I went to the same otolaryngology surgeon who had worked on my sister's peanut years before. He himself was stumped, pronounced it a polyp "not otherwise specified," and gave me some truly enormous antibiotic pills. I realized the extent of the beastie in me when, for the next week or so, I'd wake up each morning with a huge crust of pus and blood on my pillow that had drained from my ear. But I responded to these gobs of tissue, and the awareness that, untreated, the polyp could have spread to my brain, like a typical fourteen-year-old: "Cool!"

* * *

The symbolism of our different experiences with the Yale surgeon now seems so profound. Somehow, my instinctive confidence that my body would pull through is an assurance my sister has never felt. Not that she's frail or weak. In fact, she's not only strong, but also tough, both mentally and physically. But whether it's luck or constitution or reflexes or exposure or fate, my sister often has been forced to accept a sick role that is more complicated than simply receiving extra attention. She has experienced a parade of possible cancers, false positive tests, strange symptoms, and unlikely illnesses. Take, for example, our romantic escapades. On my honeymoon, I cracked open my head by accidentally hurtling into the tile wall of a swimming pool (beware free mixed drinks and a swim-up bar!) Not only did I get to play doctor and close a laceration, but I acquired a good-looking scar in the bargain, with the small cost of a sore neck. My sister jumped off our low roof to meet a boyfriend one night in high school. She broke her back.

My senior thesis in college was a cross-cultural study of pain; I began to discriminate between pain and suffering. I realized that my sicknesses, injuries, and corresponding sick roles have involved high degrees of pain with very low degrees of suffering. Indeed, I feel as if I'm not truly living if I don't sustain a basal level of pain in my daily life—pain not only from chosen activities like exercising but also the random bruises and cuts I get from being who I am.

My sister, born from the same genetic pool and raised in the same environment, has developed a very different relationship with her body and surroundings. I told my father I was thinking of writing an essay on the differences between my sister's and my experiences of being "not well." My father, an English professor who excels at recognizing complex patterns and turning them into pithy observations said, "You can live happily with a high degree of pain, perhaps too high a degree, but you have no tolerance for suffering."

I learned that my sophomore year in college. I had the silliest of minor injuries, spraining my knee doing a little drunken aikido practice in a basement hallway. The pain grew worse, and I eventually went to an orthopedic surgeon, who determined that I had torn some knee cartilage that would have to be removed. It was one of my first experiences with surgery, and I entered it a little apprehensively.

The surgery went smoothly, and the recovery was only a little challenging: crutches fit my sick role persona in that they were visible signs of my injury, but this time my persona had to adapt to a symbol that actually impeded me for a prolonged period. However, even that adaptation wasn't too difficult. The infirmity produced by the crutches was novel, and, of course, it was seen as temporary both by me and those around me.

The true challenge came a year later. When school started in the fall, my knee suddenly began to buckle. I had done nothing, and yet here my knee—*my* knee—was telling me it wasn't able to keep up. The crisis came two or three months into school when I left my room to take the short walk to a classroom immediately across the courtyard. Halfway there, my knee buckled and I almost fell.

I immediately turned around, went back to my room, skipped the class, and cried. I can't remember any sickness or physical pain that made me cry since my early teens. Now I sobbed. It was bad enough that I seemed robbed of my basic ability to bounce back from injury and overcome physical adversity. But even worse, I couldn't assign the theft to any agent beyond my own body, the vehicle for and in some ways architect of that very identity!

Everyone has a personal mythology, an autobiographical storyline. Although it may seem objectively minor, my personal mythology casts the collapse of my knee as a crisis, a tragic revelation, a monumental event of transition, aging, loss and re-evaluation. That's the thing about personal mythologies; by definition, they can be pretty melodramatic. But my overdramatic response to this injury, with its new emotional dimensions, proves my dad's point: I'm crummy at suffering. He's right—my moment of most intense suffering was merely the thought that I might become frail or impaired, a suffering that was recognizable only to myself.

Of course, such a realization can be truly devastating for certain classes of people. Now, as a working adult, I know this can be true of people who depend on physical functioning for their livelihood. Then, as an athlete, I recognized its implications for serious competitors. Around that time I talked with a collegiate varsity swimmer who was constantly injured. Together we came to understand why this particular pain caused such suffering. We agreed that, paradoxically, athletes can tolerate the most and the least pain. Workouts are often little more than a constant battle with pain: sometimes deft swordplay, sometimes sheer wrestling. But pain is not just the enemy, and at a certain level the athlete becomes a sorcerer calling up a demon. One learns to read pain, to construct from it, to incorporate and ignore and utilize it. In the process of "workouts" the athlete builds, through the manipulation and management of pain, a healthy, vital, well-oiled machine. But when the demon escapes the pentagram, pain becomes something utterly intolerable. Most people adapt to minimize the pain or capitalize on it, but athletes have a different role. Pain that sidelines an athlete isn't just an obstacle: it obliterates the individual's essence. It produces an un-athletic athlete. In such cases, the physical pain itself is almost always tolerable. It's the meaning of the pain that causes suffering: the fact that peak performance, or even any meaningful performance, is no longer possible. My buckling knee meant I might not ski, climb, weight-lift, roll, dance, jump, hike, run, play or bike without concern or inhibition ever again. I had no sick role to accommodate this. What role can you adopt when your central essence is so deeply impaired?

* * *

Recently my sister faced an analogous medical situation. For the last two years or so Katy has had intermittent Bell's palsy, which is characterized by a paralysis of one half of the face, including the mouth and eye. Her doctors disagree about its origin and treatment, and this mirrors uncertainty in the medical community in general regarding this condition.

Like my knee, the palsy strikes at the heart of her identity. Katy is a teacher, an actress, and a social genius. At twenty-three she has mastered the sensitive, nuanced arts of expression and communication. It is precisely these abilities which are threatened by the palsy. For the last half-year or more she has had no symptoms. Our hopes were growing, but this afternoon her e-mail arrived. I was wrestling with the connection between the trivial sick roles of my youth and my realization that adulthood might require developing adaptations that challenge deeper levels of self. Her note reminds me how sophisticated my little sister is, and how naive am I.

* * *

> Yeah, I have Bell's palsy again. The face is mild—it only shows when I laugh—but the fevers, sensitivity to sound, eye dryness, etc. are all up and kicking. I guess it's better this way, even though I have no visible proof of my suffering. . . .I just need to focus on eliminating stress as much as possible.
>
> Interesting that prayer seemed to help.
>
> Last night the joy of analysis was pure…and unadulterated by fear of harsh grading, etc. This may be my body's subtle reminder that the reason I'm studying lit is not for the extra two letters to my name, but to understand humanity more deeply. I was thinking about prayers, as I tried to combat the creeping paralysis, and I pulled out the truths to form my own, something like this:
>
> Whatever life-giving force is out there, be present with me as I seek through language and art to know some of the most beautiful praises by your people on earth. Later, I will share them with others, I will give strength to the weak and I will help the suffering and I will try my best to forgive others for the blows they've given and to forgive myself for the pain I've self-inflicted. Continue to give me glimpses of your beauty unveiled, and don't let me stop rejoicing in your light.
>
> This is a gift, to be here with the archaic morning bells of academia and the whispering leaves that are changing even as I am. The panic of losing those nerves again has led to a different, deeper sort of calm.
>
> thinking of you,
>
> katy

Song of Knife on Glass

Diane LeBlanc

Every day of my sadness I ate
an avocado in four slices
and set each new heart to soak.

But today the produce shelves are empty.
Only pistachios, open-mouthed and salty.

Hearts slurp and crack.
I play a knife on glass, not a tune
but a song of knife on glass.

If love brought me three pears
I'd envy their bald maps of bone.

Today's heart is a snail.
Today's water salty.

Analysis

Judith Harris

You say I have made a wall out of my life.
So, I imagine it, brick by brick,
the way clouds concretize out of vapor
as they pass, unbidden
in these interpretable woods—what languor,
what gall, to keep up that power of obstruction,
unyielding, distant as paradise—
closing out all human voices,
all golden ladders to climb up,
where the moon only frowns,
and all flowers are quick to suffocate,
as if all this time,
I could have dreamt there was another side
if I only wanted.
Wanting can be anything,
and joy, that ingenious ivy
can shatter even the hardest rock.

Restoration

Cecilie Scott

Eleventh floor: etched glass doors, art deco lounge, all quite tasteful. Magazines on the blond Parsons table, *Vogue, Elle, New Yorker,* an upscale selection replacing the non-selection of the lower level waiting rooms (Cancer Society brochures in Radiation in the basement, various Medical Center brochures in Oncology on two, outdated *People* magazines in Short Stay on five). And, wonder of wonders, windows through which we who wait can watch Seattle's pale November sun warm the gray buildings stepping down the hill to Elliott Bay. I assumed a wait and settled in, pulling a yellow pad from my backpack to note these distinctions and add this snarky comment to my journal, "Clearly I have arrived." (Like most patients, I tried to show proper attitude.)

Such elegance held more promise than actuality for the two of us in the waiting room. A frail woman in her mid-sixties had been wheeled in and parked in her chair. Neatly dressed, but definitely not *Vogue*, not *Elle*, she wore a shoe on one foot and a pink slipper on the other, and above the slipper I could see her ankle and lower leg, splotched red and cruelly scarred by burns. And me? No visible scars, but neither *Vogue* nor *Elle*, a candidate for a breast that was not a breast but a mound of silicone sheathed in muscle.

Reconstruction, like *Vogue*, deals with image. Substance—delicious nerve endings, breast as organ of perception—was no longer an issue. We wouldn't talk of such things there. Although cancer treatment redefined my body as object, artifact, and construct, I resisted as identity splintered and new patterns coalesced, for even a cyborg may feel nostalgia for a lost unity, however illusory. And yes, I knew I'd always been a part of a complex human system—never a pure child of nature.

I was led into an examining room, instructed to remove all clothes above the waist and put on a gown—opening in front this time. Dr. Z entered, android, devoid of personality. *By design, I thought, complete denial that there are two humans here, or even one.* He proceeded as if programmed. *Who could be angry or difficult here?* Anger would have bounced off his smooth surface; it was easier to join him in the fiction of objectivity.

He laid out the procedure: saline-filled implant inserted between chest muscle and rib cage, expanded with additional liquid over a period of weeks until the desired size (*Whose desire?* I wondered while nodding to show comprehension) is attained, then replaced—more surgery—with a sack of silicone gel. He listed possible complications. In ten percent of cases the muscles contract around this intrusion in the flesh and must be forced to relax their grip—more surgery. And what else? Oh yes, the other breast is lifted, its sag removed to match the firm new mound.

"And a nipple?" I asked, a knowledgeable consumer fingering the wares. I learned that after the new breast is settled into what should be its permanent position and the old one hoisted up to match, only then—all architectural remodeling completed—could we proceed to that last fillip of decoration, a nipple, or more precisely, the appearance of one.

I told him I was considering lumpectomy with radiation, and so was interested in reconstruction for future reference, just in case. I almost said, "Just looking."

"Well, after radiation, we have to use a different procedure. We can't use an implant then." He explained that bone is weakened by radiation, so expansion is inadvisable. The ribs might break before the muscle stretched enough. After radiation they use an "abdominal pouch."

"Not as satisfactory," he said. Overcoming any reluctance to discuss such shoddy wares, he described a pouch of skin and flesh slid from stomach to breast position, still attached to its own source of nourishment, rerouting vein, umbilicus for this hunk of belly reborn as breast. Not an elegant solution, he implied, leaving much to be desired in form (*and firmness*, I suspected), and sometimes this flesh, failing to thrive on alien soil, withers and dies.

Nothing he'd said made the prospect of submitting to additional surgery more appealing. Reconstruction struck me as a zipper providing permanent entry into my body to correct any future problems—medical or aesthetic. Years before I'd read Gabrielle Burton's *Heartbreak Hotel* and passed it along to my friends. We all had our favorite passages, but each of us could quote this one: "IN THE MUSEUM OF THE REVOLUTION THERE IS A TIT MEASURER. IT HAS MEASURED EVERY TIT THAT HAS EVER BEEN. EVERY ONE IS THE WRONG SIZE." [Capitalization in the original.]

Women's breasts expand with age, and nothing in Dr. Z's pitch acknowledged the likelihood that mine would too, requiring either further expense and pain to keep them even or else the use of padding to supplement his handiwork. *Vogue* and *Elle* set unattainable standards, and fashion ceases to be fun once you place cosmetic surgery on a continuum with foot binding and genital mutilation. And that was how I saw it.

By 1991, when I met with Dr. Z about this procedure, the FDA had acted in response to what were then considered well-documented cases of women injured by silicone gel leaking from breast implants into the surrounding tissue. The week before my meeting with Dr. Z in 1991, the *Seattle Post-Intelligencer* had run a feature reporting the research and discussion behind the FDA's move to limit the use of implants. When I asked Dr. Z about this, he dismissed it as a flap caused by a few troublemakers. There'd been no problems with implants themselves, he assured me. Safe enough for his wife and daughter, he said. But he did suggest I might want to take into account the possible unavailability of this option after January when making my decision. Although the article noted that the FDA had made an exception allowing the use of silicone implants for post-mastectomy reconstruction, I didn't point this out to Dr. Z. I'd had enough of him; I wanted out.

Looking back I recognize the methods of a surgeon. First anesthetize, separating flesh from feeling. Then slice through that which connects mind and body. I can understand why a surgeon might need such distancing in the operating room, but there in the examining room the claims of objectivity became tools of domination. Although I'd been living in and with my body for fifty years, my intimate knowledge, already rendered suspect by biopsy and mammogram, was irrelevant before the expertise of this professional. We were there to consider repairs required to fix a machine, a flawed machine, but one that a skilled craftsman could remake as good as new. In fact, the implication was that it would be better than new once the high, firm breasts were in place. How could any woman refuse such an offer?

Silicone, saline, belly flab, all seem indignities. I hug my other option to myself—a smooth rib cage on the right, marked only by a scar. Androgyny at last.

Feminists had raised androgyny as an option in the 1980's, but as men discovered their inner woman it became clear that male privilege would lead to male appropriation of any desirable traits previously assigned to women; the approved androgyne would continue to be male, even when the androgynous role was played by a biological female. And yet when I looked at photographs of Shiva and Parvati, seamlessly merged as one, carved in stone at the eighth century Indian temple of Elephanta, a sigh of peace rose from deep within me, my response to a nonduality that bypassed for a moment out of time all I knew of historical fact or political theory. It was this image of wholeness that sustained me then, assuring me that more than one kind of wholeness was possible, that if I had to lose a breast—and I was struggling to keep it—my revised body, reflecting Parvati's curving acquiescence on the left and Shiva's relaxed assurance on the right, would help compensate me for that loss. Not the old interpretation of Shiva incorporating Parvati, but a woman *and* a whole human being.

Androgyny was particularly appealing because the whole cancer process seemed demeaning. The Medical Center's system had been designed to guide me towards mastectomy-with-reconstruction for several possible reasons, not one of which acknowledged me as a reasonable adult.

Oh, it's so hard to allow myself to be dismembered! Yet perhaps all this concern for one admittedly small breast is a diversion, my way of avoiding the question of death.

It is believed, even stated as fact, that without the option of reconstruction we women are more likely to reject treatment, so schedulers at the Medical Center were instructed to set up appointments with a plastic surgeon for all mastectomy candidates. Medical practice in general tilts away from confusing the patient with too many choices; we're offered choices, but firmly guided towards the proper ones—for our own good. And like poets, breast cancer patients seize on metaphors, using the grammar of a body outfitted with two breasts to speak of health and wholeness, erase the shame of breast cancer (and yes, that does exist), and flip back the calendar to a time of greater innocence. The silicone pouch offered by Dr. Z was designed to carry the weight of these desires and that relocated belly fat promised a tradeoff women have been offering half-jokingly for years. The promise of a better shape after breast cancer changes the narrative to one in which the patient comes through adversity renewed, a heroine rather than a victim.

And then there's money, as reflected in that waiting room. Plastic surgeons have campaigned to bring all their procedures into the tent of medical necessity. (Even breast enlargement is covered by insurance once small breasts are defined as a deformity.) What would happen if reconstruction were not a medical necessity for every woman who has a mastectomy? Insurance companies could seize the chance to reclassify reconstruction as cosmetic surgery; no longer a covered benefit, women needing it would lose that option. And, living as we do in a world where the appearance of health and wholeness matters, this would truly be a loss. The other losers would of course be the plastic surgeons and the medical centers.

My needs, unfortunately, could not be met by reconstruction. I wanted to preserve my breast because it was part of me, not because I needed the appearance of wholeness. If I had to lose my breast, I'd still insist that reconstruction was not restoration and therefore not my route towards wholeness.

My stomach unclenched and the colors of fall dazzled my eyes as I walked downhill from the Medical Center towards the bay. With each step upon the pavement I felt the earth supporting me all the way down to its core. I stopped at a Belltown café to wait for Frank. (My husband, an actor, had a rehearsal in a storefront on the other side of Second Avenue.) From my table I could look out through French doors to a patio tucked into the gap between buildings. The last light of day washed the stucco wall to the south with sunset shades, glowing pale rose to ruddy gold, slowly fading as I watched; three slender saplings, springing from the red brick paving, darkened from silvery green to leaden gray silhouettes against the wall. Fourteen years later a fine young cherry tree lights the wall with blossoms in the spring, its roots spreading through the hidden soil, finding sustenance, drinking in the rain that seeps between the bricks.

My left breast remains, my right side smooth save for a crescent scar that marks the year that I had cancer. When I step from the shower I see three turtles surfing the waves that rise from the bottom of my ribs to curl and foam at the tip of my shoulder. Like *Vogue* and *Elle*, I acknowledge that appearance matters. Mine shows the path taken among those offered. I thought that I was choosing then but now believe each step was determined by what was possible for me—at that time, in that place, living in that body. I smile at my reflection as the mist on the mirror clears. I am alive, and the turtles celebrate life, as encouraging and improbable as the tree that springs from the narrow carpet of bricks spread between those Belltown buildings.

Fever

Mary Kathryn Jablonski

Lights stay on all night. Refrigerator
noise becomes a knock you struggle to
ignore, then want to answer but cannot. Snow
no longer is an outdoor phenomenon.
You dust away a pile to find your keys.
Curved marble doors, light as wafers,
open to nursery after nursery
connected by dark wet stairs. You search for
a place to vomit a mouthful of cured
meat. You're walking along a highway that
suddenly becomes a lake of loons and
in a field beyond, deer whisper. As they
turn away, you follow, mesmerized, catch
yourself falling from the edge of a cliff
and realize: this landscape is moving,
a great fevered beast asleep, stretching.

Formula

Cheryl Stiles

Wing of a tree-toad frog
fire coral
Sargasso reed
Blowfish burn
heart slowed
breath gone
Unearth this wooden
bonebox break
loose its bitter seed

Message

Toward the pond
rye grasses slope their seedpods.
An inchworm drops
onto my notebook,
curves to a Chinese character—
calligraphic, almost oracular.

It furthers one to cross the great water.

Sutures

Karen Holmberg

The woman on the other side
of emergency's curtain groaned
my babies   my babies
as a specially muffled drone imparted
the bad news, and I saw beyond the hem

the blunt hands of her feet
clinging and rubbing, grey heels
cracked like abandoned dough, ankles
traversed by puffy rivers, while
on our side with tender precision

the doctor dipped the curved needle
to close the curtain on
my toddler's skull, setting to the side
tremulous sympathy
as the small body called out urgently

for repair. For my love could not
help it. When I'd raised
the corner of the towel limp
and leaden with her blood and saw
gold seed-pearls of fat, and beneath them

the clean-sheared edges of her meat
opening on the bluish skull, gleaming
and plastic, my body urged me
to cover the wound's lips
with my lips *flesh*

of my flesh as if I could be
a human suture beyond the needs
of food or water, speech or air.

Her face was draped and cross-
draped in blue. I had access
only to one fixed and anxious eye, so I whispered

into its dark unfurnished room
our next day's trip to my childhood
home, setting afloat
a boat with a green and yellow sail, reaching
her hand into leaves

for the peaches she could pick
and eat
Where is this paradise
our doctor murmured while she lay
a track with filament so fine
the wrists revolving, throwing loops for

glinting tools to shoot through
seemed pure pantomime. And yet
the wound drew closed
as I watched, submitting to
those intricate continuous knots.

Morning Tapestry: A Sonata of Pain

Laurie Lessen-Reiche

I'm not not in my body
I'm everywhere else but not in my body not in my head
I'm everywhere dispersed still dreaming still hoping for
healing sleep not asleep or dreaming I'm scattered
splattered like roughed-up particles like the devastation the
bombed-out hut of metaphor the simile tinder the seed-
feathers floating the teardrop flux the ache of
cancer with its elegiac sonata of pain not here but spun
from rafter to rafter like like (!) cotton-candy webbing and
rosy shadows: the stain of the hymen coral-pink and
plundered torn asunder
blush of splayed labia me hiding in my own
vagina little cave of surrender sea-cove-synagogue
domed cathedral amnesty-nest place of internment
place of rest port of rendezvous port of prayer poet's
hospice me bowed on a cervical mattress
un-done and re-becoming dissolving and bonding
in the cellular surf heaving and swelling surging
in the paramecium sea dreaming cohesion
dreaming being weaving
and singing

Saving Amy

Tammy Wilson

Wilford Evans pants at the front porch screen, desperate, like a wild dog ready to leap through it. "Mr. Roland! Help!"

Glazed in fear, his wife Della stands behind him with her hair clinched in a ponytail, cradling their young daughter in a wrinkled pink nightgown. The child's eyes are rolled back, her cheeks flushed.

Hugh Roland jolts from his evening newspaper and calls through the screen to the couple huddled there on the porch.

"What's wrong?" he says.

He has met them only once, when he was out mowing last spring. He usually hires a kid instead of marching his fifty-year-old bones around the yard, but with polio raging, few care to venture out this summer. After seeing their battered Studebaker rumble into the lawn of the rental house across the road, Hugh strode over to meet the latest in the series of temporary neighbors. The Evanses, barely in their twenties, seemed as if they were doing him a favor to offer so much as a neighborly handshake. He remembers their names—Della and Wilford—clumsy old-fashioned names that don't fit their young faces.

"Our Amy's sick. We got to get her to the hospital and our car's broke down."

Wilford's voice is brittle. He has never seen his child so desperately sick.

The news about the car is no surprise. He has wondered for weeks how their old sedan has managed to clunk along. Like so many others, the Evanses live from hand to mouth, paycheck to paycheck, and when bad luck hits, they haunt his front porch, begging for their share of the county dole. He's seen it all too many times, and he wonders why he hangs on as commissioner, having to deal with such people. As township commissioner, it's his habit to keep track and to make things even and familiar, particularly when election time rolls around. Usually he's more mindful about who moves into that little clapboard house, but the kind of people who rent it don't stay long. Like flighty birds, they barely set up their nest and they're gone—rent past due, potential votes wasted. He wishes he could buy the house and control who lives there, but it belongs to a widow who won't sell, even though it's been skinned and cobbled beyond recognition.

Now their limping vehicle has quit, and they're stranded at the worst possible moment as their little girl burns with fever. He has seen the curly-haired child before, alone on the porch swing and riding her bicycle with training wheels dangerously close to the road and wondered how she has survived without a calamity, though such people seem to scrape by in spite of their poor judgment.

Once, on the way to town, he stopped and rolled down his window. "Does your mother know you're out here?"

The little girl shrugged and teetered back toward the driveway, no more than a couple of ruts skidding to the shade of an ailing Dutch elm. He could see Della Evans peer suspiciously out the front door with her hair up in bobby pins.

"Your little girl was way out by the road," he called.

Without a thank-you, the young woman stormed down the front steps, snapped a branch off the forsythia, and began shouting threats at the child. Mothers like that aren't fit to raise children, he thought, but he seems to see more of them every day, especially the ones who come to his door for handouts.

Standing before him now, Della Evans appears drenched in nervous perspiration, her voice begging. "We can't break the fever and the Doc says get her to the hospital right away."

"And now our car won't start. Oh God, can you help us?" Her husband runs his hand over the top of his bristly crew cut.

"Meet me around back," Hugh sounds mechanical, as if he's making a campaign promise. He grabs his hat as he runs through the house, quickly tells his wife, Joan, where he's going. She is busy peeling potatoes into the kitchen sink. She looks up, startled. "You don't think it could be. . . ."

Infantile paralysis is stalking their part of Illinois. Like any scourge, it makes no distinctions among who it strikes, and now it's found its way up their road and has the audacity to knock at their own front door. She scurries to the linen closet to hand him a pale blue blanket used when their sons were young.

"For the back seat," she says.

He appreciates her thoughtfulness. He pecks her on the cheek before he dashes down the back steps, nearly stumbling over his own feet.

The Evanses are waiting desperately beside his shiny white Buick. Hugh quickly spreads the blanket before Wilford helps Della and the little Amy into the back seat. He hopes the girl won't soil his new upholstery. He wastes no motions backing the car out the drive and onto the road toward town and swerves around two chuckholes before accelerating down a straight country road, part of the checkerboard landscape of corn and soybean fields.

"She got real hot all of a sudden," Wilford says. "We put her in a tub of cold water, but that didn't help none. Then we called the doctor and he said to bring her in as soon as we could."

He sounds like any father trying to do whatever it takes to save his child, though Hugh can't remember much about those days. Joan always got up in the middle of the night when Frank, Steve or Joey was sick.

"Please, baby, wake up!" Della's voice cracks.

Hugh presses forward. "Has she been around any sick kids?"

"None I know of," Wilford answers. "She ain't gone swimming or nothing and school doesn't start for another week. She'll be in second grade," he says hopefully.

The Rolands have raised three respectable sons, who have seen their share of scrapes, broken bones and childhood catastrophes, but Joan always tended to the boys.

He has never had to deal with an emergency like this one. He feels as if he's watching himself. He has feared the polio outbreak since the first case was confirmed, and, as the summer dragged into August, more children have become ill, like in the old days, when typhoid and diphtheria stalked farms and crossroads. Now parents ponder iron lungs and crutches instead of caskets and lamb-shaped monuments. They consider the cost of treatment, scrape and borrow, take public aid if they have to. When it comes to a scourge like this one, it's everybody's business.

"We can only hope and pray for the best," Wilford says. He grips the door handle as the car makes a sharp turn onto the blacktop.

In his haste, Hugh happens to notice his gas gauge and eases up on the pedal, swearing under his breath. "Out of gas!"

"Oh Lord, what are we going to do?" Della cries from the back seat.

"We're going to have to stop someplace and quick," Hugh says.

As the Evanses breathe panicked moans, he searches the horizon and the rearview mirror for the nearest farmhouse. All farmers keep gasoline on hand to fuel their machinery.

He spots a familiar hip-roofed barn.

"Let's try Old Man Ripley's," Hugh says.

It's the last place he wants to stop. During the last election, Charlie Ripley refused to let him tack campaign signs on his property. But today Hugh has no choice. He spins the car around in the middle of the road and in a swirl of dust he pulls his tires onto the gravel, lurches to a halt and rushes to the gas pump. Wilford unscrews the gas cap. The pump spits, then starts rattling precious fuel in a low hum.

"We'll just put in enough to get to town. I'll settle up with them later," Hugh says.

"Oh please hurry," Della calls pitifully. "Her breath's getting shallower."

As the dial registers the second gallon, the pump suddenly shudders and falls silent. Hugh swears and looks up.

A severe-looking woman in thick glasses appears on the back porch with both hands on her hips. Her feisty dog yips its way the edge of the porch and growls hesitation on the top step. "What do you think you're doing?"

Wilford steps toward her, raising his palms with each step. "It's an emergency, Ma'am. We got to get to the hospital."

"You going to pay me for the gas you stole?" She flaps her arms like wings.

Charlie Ripley and his wife aren't the sort to lend anything, not even a couple gallons of gas, and his wife is no exception. Childless and selfish, the couple has made a thorny bed to lie in.

"I'm Hugh Roland, Mrs. Ripley. Tell Charlie I'll settle up with him later. We've got to get a little girl to the hospital."

The brown feist snaps an incessant high-pitched yap.

Mrs. Ripley grabs a shovel propped against the porch wall. "Hugh Roland don't have no girl." She's already at the bottom of the porch steps, pointing the spade at them.

"Get back in the car," he tells Wilford.

As both men scramble into the front seat, the old woman shakes her fist saying something they can't hear. The tires spin out of the gravel as the feist bounds toward them.

"Hold on," Hugh says, zooming around a slow-moving load of hay. Why must farmers rule the road at times like this? He swerves dangerously close to the culverts as he pulls onto the main highway, speeding past the drive-in theater and the grain elevator before reaching the outskirts of town. The county hospital rises out of the flat fields like a marble monument to modern marvels. Luckily none of his family has been sick enough or hurt badly enough to darken its doors since the boys were born. Healthy strapping boys. It's outrageous to imagine them otherwise.

Hugh wheels under a brick canopy marked "emergency," then he and the three Evanses burst into the emergency room. Hugh flags a nurse who quickly moves them behind a cubicle, yanking a blue curtain around them. A doctor frowns over little Amy's body. Hugh stays with the parents until the child can be assigned to an isolation unit. Fevers are serious business and no one wants to take any chances. He wonders how he will disinfect his new car, if indeed Amy Evans has polio, and he thinks how Joan will set bleach to the blanket, twist it in her own hands before cranking it through the wringer. Probably she will ruin it getting the germs out, and then hang it in the sun to dry, but it will still be tainted. Maybe he'll burn it.

"Thank God you got here before the fever got any worse," the doctor says.

Hugh touches the doctor's sleeve, almost apologetically. "The parents. I'm not sure they'll be able to pay."

The physician purses his lips and shakes his head. "We take quite a few county cases."

Hugh knows that's what the county coffers are for, cases like this one. Through a slit in the curtain, he sees that Della has assumed a vigil at her daughter's bedside, her gaze fixed on the ill child weighted with cold packs and covered in a shroud of white cotton, her sweaty curls barely visible. Tubing coils from a glass bottle perched high overhead as yellow light bathes her in an artificial glow.

Wilford steps out toward him and shakes his hand. "I don't know what we would've done without you."

They embrace, like a father and son, though he doesn't remember the last time he held his own sons so tightly.

The sun sets as Hugh heads home, stopping at a service station to wash his hands as fifteen gallons of ethyl quench his thirsty tank. As he heads back down the hard road, he knows he must stop at the Ripleys and pay for the precious fuel he "borrowed." He'll tell them that the little Evans girl is safe in the hospital. Maybe Mrs. Ripley will calm down when she hears that. But as he approaches their stretch of road, he sees a figure near the ditch. It is Mrs. Ripley kneeling, her hands over her ears. He stops the car and walks toward her as she wails over body of her little dog reduced to skinned meat.

"Skip! Skip!" Her hair is frenzied like a brush pile in a winter storm. Tears glisten her leathery cheeks. "Seven years we had him. Only seven years."

"It's a shame." He never knows what to say at times like this. To Mrs. Ripley, the dog is probably the closest thing to a child, the nearest thing to her heart. He tries to imagine the pain the old woman is feeling, the pain of what it would be like if he lost one of his sons, pain the Evanses will feel if Amy takes a turn for the worse.

"He didn't stop," she whimpers, wringing her hands as if to wash them.

"Who?"

"The gas truck. He was hit by a gas truck."

He stands there with Mrs. Ripley as cruel justice seeps over him. The precious fuel she accused him of stealing is somehow responsible for killing the one thing she held dear.

He clears his throat. "I'll get a shovel."

He doesn't want to touch the dead animal, but it's the only decent thing to do. He knows exactly where to look for the garden tool, and when he retrieves it from the porch, he leaves a fifty-cent piece, way more than enough for the gas, and leaves it under a spare brick that must be the doorstop. It seems so little to pay for something that meant so much, but it doesn't matter now. Time has already marched into something else.

When he returns to the roadside, Mrs. Ripley is still kneeling beside her pet, wailing as if ready to rend her clothing. Death has come quickly where blood forms round puddle on the asphalt. Reluctantly, he picks up the stiffening animal, and lays him onto the grass.

"Charlie will be home." She wrestles the shovel from him. "No use to do any more."

"I can bury him. Show me where."

She turns away and heads toward the house. The dog, glassy-eyed and silent, lies as he has laid him. Flies start to gather on the skinned flanks and up where blood oozes onto the brittle, sun-baked blades of grass.

"I left some money on the back porch," he calls after her. "Mrs. Ripley?" but the old woman was walking toward the house.

Yolanda Tooley ~ *Cicero Porch*

Falls

Allan Peterkin

How would you feel if your therapist stole your life and then won a Pulitzer Prize for writing about it?

I told Dr. Peterzill what happened when my husband and I went to Niagara Falls that first day of spring. It had been one of my assignments in therapy. To do something lovey-dovey with Joe, as things had been different since the kids left home. Our routine was gone and Joe was having prostate problems (not cancer, thank God). I was off my estrogen after that cancer scare in the news. It all felt like a turning point, and it made me nervous. Joe didn't put up a fuss about going, though. I bought us new spring clothes—a yellow sweater set for me and a navy blue Nautica sweater for him. We had blueberry waffles at Denny's the morning we arrived and strolled the town hand in hand. We didn't have lunch, but went back to the hotel room for a nap. We cuddled, but neither one of us made the move towards...intimacy. Maybe after a good supper and a few Seabreezes, our favorite drink, I thought. That was my assignment, after all.

We got up and drove to the falls to refresh ourselves before a late dinner. The mist was supposed to be good for you—all those negative ions have a positive effect on the brain. (Hoped it wasn't the other way around.) Anyway, you could smell them just like you can smell a storm coming.

Ice had given way to flow.
There were chunky, crashing sounds.
A red-pinkish light had
stolen the sky.

There weren't many people at that time of day. There were day people and night people and this was somehow in between. And there we were, holding hands right at the spot where

the calm shelf of water became violent,
where everything gets carried downward
in those crashing, thundering falls.

Gave me that butterfly feeling in my stomach, and I had to step back from the rail. And then we saw her. A woman in a red sequin dress floating on her back.

She was not moving, her arms were extended straight out from her shoulders. No backstroke. No flailing. Nothing. And the water so terribly cold. Joe and I couldn't move either, couldn't even call for help.

She floated closer towards us and, my God, towards the edge. She looked at each of us right in the eye, and we both turned to stone. This was not a goodbye to strangers. She was heading towards the precipice. It would be seconds, and her face was blank except for those eyes fixed now, only on Joe. I started hyperventilating. Tears fell from my eyes. But I couldn't close them.

Then she went over
without any human sound.
A doomed red vessel.

Joe grabbed his chest and crumpled to the ground. I still couldn't move, but somebody saw what happened and came over. He called 911 on his cell phone. The ambulance came. Joe had had the first of his heart attacks. More would come, but he survived that first one.

They found the woman, they said, only because of her red dress. She had run out of the casino at twilight and jumped. She had lost her house, pension, her kids' college fund. Apparently it happens more than the public knows,

the dark secret
of that tourist town.

I kept seeing that red dress and those eyes. For months. But I couldn't give into it because of Joe. Dr. Peterzill kept asking me over and over to describe what happened. Every single detail. Colors. Smells. What my body felt. De-programming trauma, he called it.

And then his book came out, called *Falls.*

Every poem had the color red in it.

I Am No More or Less

Sarah Jefferis

If I brought you my breasts on a platter
you would pour sauce on them before you sliced them;
you'd know I was as gentle as St. Agatha
who carried her pomegranates on silver
after the Roman soldiers plucked them.

But you would deem them vile,
paint them with arsenic, or mercury,
wrap them in tobacco plants
and rotten apples, or even compresses soaked
in cow urine and live pigeons severed in half.

You'd call me a witch,
sever off my own flesh and force it
in the mouths of my sons as they watch me flame.

So I will draw my flesh out of your mouth
and spill the second Milky Way into the ocean.
They cannot make you immortal.

Ichthyosis

Gina Liotta

she is naked, still in pain
the sheets greased with Vaseline
and epidermal debris
                                        her pubic hairs
withering in her desert encasement

the skin on her legs is raised
cornmeal colored layer flakes
in the shape of Pangaea
            blood rivers
pouring down the slopes as the continents shift

my father sits next to her as she cries
silently holding her hand
i used to think he was the brave one
to marry my mother, have sex
with my mother, make babies with
my mother, stay with my mother

but in her most painful moments
she is the brave one to allow someone
to watch her breathe and decay
invite him into her body—knowing

To Someone Who Asked Me After a Poetry Reading How To "Make It" in Poetry

Bruce Bennett

I should have told you, "There's no easy way.
You just persist, and do it on your own."
I failed you, though; I didn't know what to say.

You waited, eager-eyed; you clearly stay
hungry for gleanings, desperate to be shown.
I should have told you, "There's no easy way.

You write and write and write, and then one day—
or not—you gather fruit from what you've sown."
Some such old saw. I didn't know what to say,

Because I don't. You struggle, and you pray,
and give it all you've got, and work alone,
and learn quite early there's no easy way

And maybe none at all, but that's okay,
because it's what you choose, and it's the on-
ly thing you want to do. What can one say?

You have this one compulsion. You obey.
You roll your rock. It rolls back down. You groan.
I should have told you, "There's no easy way."
I failed you, though; I didn't know what to say.

Pamela Ferris-Olson ~ *Seafarer's Gossamer*

Contributors

Katie Antony is a third-year medical student at the University of Rochester School of Medicine and Dentistry. Her pieces have appeared in *Blood and Thunder* and *Neurology*, and she has a piece forthcoming in *The Fox Cry Review*. Last summer her poem "How to Fix" won the 2006 Michael E. DeBakey Medical Student Poetry Award.

Sarah Averill was born in Bangor, Maine, and grew up in Mexico and Upstate New York. As an undergraduate at Cornell University she studied the history of women and work. She then went on to receive a master's degree in Urban and Regional Planning from the University of Iowa. She now lives with her husband and two children in Syracuse where she is a second-year medical student at SUNY Upstate Medical University.

Sara Baker teaches writing at the Loran Smith Center for Cancer Support in Athens, Georgia. Her work has appeared most recently in *Ars Medica* and the *Yale Journal for Humanities in Medicine*. She has pioneered the Woven Dialog Writing Workshop, details of which can be found on her website: www.saratbaker.com

Bruce Bennett is the author of seven books of poetry and numerous poetry chapbooks. He is Chair of English and Director of Creative Writing at Wells College in Aurora, New York. He is very pleased to have work once again in *The Healing Muse.*

Beverly Boyd is a former English teacher who lives on the central coast of California. Her poems have appeared in *English Journal, California Quarterly, THEMA,* and other journals. This is her second appearance in *The Healing Muse.*

Terri Brown-Davidson received the 2007 New Mexico Writer's Scholarship and her first book of poetry, *The Carrington Monologues*, was nominated for the Pulitzer Prize. She lives with her husband and daughter in Albuquerque and is earning her green belt in karate.

Lorraine Bruno Arsenault is a native of Canastota, New York. She is author of *The Long Run Home*, a member of the Canastota Writers Group, and a yoga instructor.

Melissa Cloonan, as a second-year medical student, was the pharmacy coordinator for the Summer Migrant Farmers' Clinic. "Wednesday Night" is a reflection about one of the farms she visited and the challenges that she encountered as a coordinator as well as her perspective on the challenges faced by the migrant workers themselves.

Daniel Corrie's poetry has appeared in *The American Scholar, Hudson Review, The Nation, Shenandoah*, and *Southern Review*. He lives in Atlanta where he works as a freelance writer and editor in the field of family crisis intervention.

Sarah Cross received her medical degree from the University of Chicago-Pritzker School of Medicine. She is currently a resident in Obstetrics & Gynecology at Yale-New Haven Hospital. Her work has been published in the *Journal of Medical Humanities, The New Physician*, and *The Legible Script*.

Brock Dethier teaches at Utah State University, has published poems in more than two dozen journals, and has written several books on teaching composition. He underwent treatment for cancer of the neck in 2004.

Lois Dorschel is secretary for the Center for Bioethics and Humanities at SUNY Upstate Medical University. Her outside interests include retreating to her cabin deep in the forest with her husband Marty and sharing life with her three wonderful sons and grandson.

Beth H. Evans lives in Ithaca, New York, and is Senior Editor for PenWorks Publishers, INC. Her novel, *The Watering Hole*, published by Penworks, INC., will be available by the end of 2007.

Elisabeth Farrell holds an M.F.A. from the Bennington Writing Seminars, where she was Jane Kenyon Scholar. Her work has been published in *Color Wheel*.

Pamela Ferris-Olson is a freelance writer and photographer who lives in Southwestern Ohio. While her photographic eye is captivated by the diversity of color and pattern that exists in the natural world, her poetic eye is focused on the intricacies of relationships. Pam is once again honored to have her work published in *The Healing Muse*.

Anetha Frasier is a graduate student in Information Studies at Syracuse University and works part-time at SUNY Upstate Medical University in Student Affairs.

M. Frost pursues her master's degree in public health when she isn't writing poetry. Her work appears in numerous journals, including *Nimrod, American Poetry Journal, Potomac Review*, and previous issues of *The Healing Muse*. Finishing Line Press published her first chapbook, *Cow Poetry and other notes from the field*, in 2006. www.mfrostwords.com

Vishwas R. Gaitonde, who holds degrees in medicine and journalism, is the author of *A Thief in the Night: Understanding AIDS*, published by East-West Books, Chennai (Madras), India. His articles, essays, and fiction have appeared in various publications in the United States, Great Britain, and India. He is a medical communications specialist based in San Diego.

Ellen Giraud was born in a small lake-side town in the northern Adirondack Mountains. She has always had a great love of animals and the outdoors. She works in the Department of Emergency Medicine at SUNY Upstate Medical University and is a manager of the Central New York Ronald McDonald House. In her free time though, she likes to quiet things down a bit, and is rarely seen without a camera to her eye—capturing those magical little moments found only in nature.

Kathleen Gunton teaches creative writing and is a professional photographer in Orange, CA.

Alexander Douglas Grant was born and raised on the Jersey Shore and has spent most of his adult life in New York City. He lives with his wife and four children in the South Bronx.

Kathleen Grieger lives in Menomonee Falls, Wisconsin. She has finished a book of poetry based on brain surgeries; the poems are being used to teach doctors that patients are people first. Her work has been published in *Caduceus, Avocet, Blood and Thunder,* and others.

William Hahn is a fourth-year medical student from Syracuse, New York. He has extensive experience working in Guatemala, both on archaeological digs and in the public health sector.

Judith Harris is the author of *Atonement: Poems* (LSU Press, 2000), *The Bad Secret: Poems* (LSU Press, 2006) and a critical book, *Signifying Pain: Constructing and Healing the Self through Writing* (SUNY Press, 2003). Her poems have appeared in *Ploughshares, The American Scholar, Prairie Schooner, The Southern Review*, and *Antioch Review,* among others.

Seth Collings Hawkins is an emergency physician and writer living in the foothills of North Carolina. This piece was written ten years ago while he was a medical student and was founder and editor of *iris*: the UNC journal of medicine, literature, and visual art. His sister earned her doctorate in comparative literature and now lives in Philadelphia, where she continues to be eerily insightful, wise beyond her age, and adamant that she will not drink cod liver oil.

Dotty Holcomb Doherty is a freelance writer living in Annapolis, Maryland. Her essays and feature stories appear regularly in the local publications *Bay Weekly* and *What's Up? Annapolis*. Her hobbies include bird watching and photographing wildflowers.

Karen Holmberg's first book, *The Perseids*, was published by the University of North Texas Press in 2001. A Discovery/The Nation award winner, her work has appeared in such magazines as *The Paris Review, The Nation, Slate, Quarterly West*, and *Southern Poetry Review*. She lives in Corvallis, Oregon.

Joyce Holmes McAllister is retired after thirty years at Cornell University as a registrar, and has been pursuing her first love, poetry. She has been published on Gratefulness.org and in *The Comstock Review*, as well as in local newsletters and newspapers.

Mehr-Afarin Hosseini is a second-year medical student at SUNY Upstate Medical University. Born in Tehran, Iran, her family moved to Toronto when she was sixteen. There she attended the University of Toronto and graduated with a B.S. in psychology. She has published stories in Farsi and English.

Whitney Howe graduated from Syracuse University in December 2006 with a degree in English and textual studies. She recently completed an internship at Bentley-Hall, Inc. in Syracuse, New York. Her work has appeared in *The International Musician* and *Making Music Magazine*. She has aspirations of working the book publishing industry and is making a move to New York City this fall. Her love of writing stems from her mother, whom she considers to be greatest supporter.

Mary Kathryn Jablonski is a visual artist/poet who serves as a gallerist at Skidmore College in Saratoga Springs, New York, and dresses mannequins. Her work will appear in the summer 2007 issue of the *Beloit Poetry Journal,* and she is completing final edits on her first book-length collection of poems, whose focus is the night sky.

Anne Jacobson Ryan is a retired art teacher who writes poems and paints. She lives in the Endless Mountains of Pennsylvania with her husband and her cat. Her poems have appeared in *Bloodroot* and *Plum Series*.

Sarah Jefferis is currently a doctoral candidate in the Department of English at Binghamton University. Her poems have appeared in *The Cream City Review*, Accomplice.org, *The Hollins Critic, The Comstock Review, The Mississippi Review, Icon, Icarus, The New Coin, The Beacon Street Review*, and *The Naughyde Literary Journal.* She is also a lecturer in women's studies at Wells College in Aurora, New York. She lives with her partner and toddler in Ithaca, New York.

Rick Kempa teaches writing and philosophy at Western Wyoming College in Rock Springs, Wyoming. His work has appeared in numerous journals and anthologies including, most recently, *ARS Medica, Bellowing Ark, Chrysalis Reader, JAMA*, and *Pilgrimage*.

Sarah Kuhlman received her A.B. in philosophy from Oberlin College and her M.D. from the University of Oklahoma. For the past fifteen years, she and her husband have lived and raised three children in Springfield, Missouri, where she has practiced neonatology.

Pamela L. Laskin is a lecturer in the English Department at The City College and director of The Poetry Outreach Center. One volume of poetry; four poetry chapbooks; two young adult novels; five picture books; and hundreds of her poems and short stories have been published.

Diane LeBlanc is the author of *Hope in Zone Four,* a poetry chapbook. Her poetry and prose appear in *Bellingham Review, Earth's Daughters, Natural Bridge, Rhino, So to Speak, Teachers & Writers, Water~Stone*, and other journals. Diane directs the writing program at St. Olaf College, where she teaches writing, women's studies, and book arts.

Laurie Lessen-Reiche lives, reads and reads and reads and writes in Novato, California. When her health permits it, she attends Dominican University of California pursuing her B.A./M.A. in Humanities with a writing emphasis. Her work has appeared in numerous magazines. She was the 2006 winner of the Charlotte Newberger Award for Poetry.

Gina Liotta holds a master's in English from Syracuse University and a master's in Middle/Secondary Education from the University of Oregon. She has published poetry and essays in *LIPS, She's Aloud: A Journal of Feminist Literature*, and the *Ugly Poets Anthology*. Gina lives in Eugene, Oregon, and teaches advanced English at Oak Hill School.

Susannah M. Loiselle was born in Syracuse, New York and attended Syracuse University, University of Michigan, and takes classes at Wells College. She and her husband raised five children near Locke, New York. Her poems and essays have been published in *The Wells Chronicle, Reflections Journal* (NC), *The Healing Muse*, and a poem will be published in the 5/08 issue of *By-Line*. Her poem, "Seacaucus, New Jersey" was included in the Susquehanna River Watershed Anthology. Her chapbook, *God Speaks to Me at the Salvation Army Thrift Store*, was published in 2004.

Susan Luzzaro has published two books of poetry and is presently at work on a book of nonfiction. She has received numerous awards for her writing including the Los Angeles Arts Council Scholarship Award, Associated Writing Programs Intro Award, Full Scholarship to Breadloaf Writers' Conference, and Santa Cruz National Writers Union's First Place Award. She is the conservator for her disabled brother and a strong advocate for her disabled sister. She is a member of the California State Council on Disabilities. She lives in Chula Vista, California, with her family.

Reneé Mezza works at SUNY Upstate Medical University in the Department of Neuroscience and Physiology. Her hobbies include photography, baking, gardening and painting.

Marilyn R. Mumford writes poetry, short fiction, and humorous nonfiction. She is an active member of the Center for Creative Retirement in Charleston, South Carolina. She's the co-founder of a women's book group in central Pennsylvania that will celebrate its twenty-fifth anniversary in 2008.

Robin Nagowski is a third-year medical student at SUNY Upstate Medical University who has always been a fan of literature and is very pleased to be a part of *The Healing Muse*. She always looks forward to free time to read and share books with friends, and now looks forward to writing about her experiences as she begins to encounter patients. She wants to thank Dr. Deirdre Neilen and Dr. Ruth Hart for encouraging the busy medical students to take time to appreciate the humanities, which makes medicine and life more enjoyable.

Robert Nazarene is founding editor of *Margie/The American Journal of Poetry.* His collection of poems is *CHURCH* (IntuiT House Poetry Series, 2006). His work has appeared in *Beloit Poetry Journal, Callaloo, Ploughshares,* and *Prairie Schooner.*

Barbara Nevaldine is a graduate of Syracuse University and has been a research associate in the Department of Radiation Oncology at SUNY Upstate Medical University for over thirty years. She enjoys gardening and nature photography.

Sarah Nicolai is a fourth-year medical student at SUNY Upstate who plans to enter Internal Medicine. She enjoys film, dance, and watching hockey with her husband, David.

Allan Peterkin is a Toronto psychiatrist and writer, and a founding editor of *ARS MEDICA: A Journal of Medicine, the Arts and Humanities.* He is completing a collection of short fiction.

Nicole Peyrafitte is a multimedia performance artist. As an autodidact, she considers each step of her work an attempt to fulfill her compulsion to learn through a process of immersion that generates performances incorporating voice/paintings/videos/writing and often cooking. www.nicolepeyrafitte.com

Maureen Picard Robins is a literacy staff developer in New York City. Her poems are from an unpublished manuscript, *The Transmigration of Souls.*

Andrea Potos's full-length collection of poems *Yaya's Cloth* was published this year by Iris Press (irisbooks.com). Her work appears widely in journals and anthologies. She lives in Madison, Wisconsin, and works as a bookseller at A Room of One's Own Feminist Bookstore.

Deborah Rexine is a sixteen-year veteran photographer in SUNY Upstate Medical University's medical photography department. She resides in Syracuse, New York, with her husband and fraternal twins. Her hobbies include photography and working with stained glass.

Oliver Rice has received the Theodore Roethke Prize and was twice featured on *Poetry Daily.* His poems appear in three recent anthologies: *Ohio Review's New and Selected, Introduction to Literature*, and Billy Collins's *180 More.* He resides in Naples, Florida.

Jennifer Richter is a former Wallace Stegner Fellow and Jones Lecturer in Poetry at Stanford University. Her poems have appeared in many national publications, including *Poetry, Ploughshares, Crab Orchard Review, Puerto del Sol,* and *A Fierce Brightness: Twenty-five Years of Women's Poetry,* published by CALYX Books.

Benita Rogers was a dancer and actress, raised a family, conducted a ballet school, and was a painter and later a stone sculptor. She is an active advocate for nature preservation. Benita is an avid writer of both prose and poetry.

Rokhsanna Sadeghi is a second-year medical student at SUNY Upstate Medical University. She received her B.S. in biochemistry/biophysics at Rensselaer Polytechnic Institute in 2006 and enjoys playing soccer, outdoor sports, dancing, and traveling.

Cecilie Scott edits to eat and lives to write in Portland, Oregon. Current projects include a memoir of travels through cancer and Bali and a story collection about travelers seeking paradise. Her work appears in *The Dos Passos Review* and *The Raven Chronicles.*

Mark J. Sicherman, M.D., is a semi-retired physician specializing in alternative and complementary medicine. He also teaches meditation to individuals and groups. His short stories have appeared previously in *The Healing Muse* and in two anthologies.

Cheryl Stiles lives in the Atlanta area and works as a university librarian. Her poems have appeared in journals such as *Atlanta Review, Poet Lore, Storysouth*, and *The Healing Muse.*

Dr. Chris Anne Strickling is the director of Texas's own and only crip theater with attitude, an ensemble performance company of disabled adults in Austin, Texas, known as *Actual Lives.* As an independent scholar, she writes about the intersections of disability, autobiography, and performance. Her relationships with the disabled adults in *Actual Lives* have completely rearranged her perspectives on almost everything.

Robertina Szolarova, R.N., B.S.N., is an alumna of SUNY Upstate's College of Nursing. She lives and writes in beautiful Sonoma, California, and works as Team Supervisor for Hospice By The Bay. The stories she encounters through her work continue to inspire her writing.

Yolanda Tooley is a professional photographer who works out of her studio in Cicero, NY. She has exhibited her work extensively, including Syracuse's Everson Museum, Chicago's Womanmade Gallery, Rochester's Memorial Art Gallery, and Washington DC's Sumner Art Museum.

Eileen Valinoti is a registered nurse. Her essays have appeared in professional nursing journals and in popular magazines such as *Glamour, Health,* and *Parents.* She lives with her family in New Jersey.

Gary Weinstein is a social worker at SUNY Upstate Hospital in Syracuse, New York, and a freelance writer.

Tammy Wilson has lived more than half her life in North Carolina, where she was a 2002 Blumenthal Writer. Her stories have most recently appeared in *Pedestal Magazine, Pisgah Review*, and *Crossroads: A Southern Culture Annual.*

Valerie Wohlfeld's collection, *Thinking the World Visible* (Yale University Press, 1994) won the Yale Series of Younger Poets Prize. Her poems have appeared recently, or are forthcoming in: *Antioch Review, Yale Review, New England Review, Prairie Schooner, Journal of the American Medical Association, Louisiana Literature, Sou'wester,* and *Southern Humanities Review.*

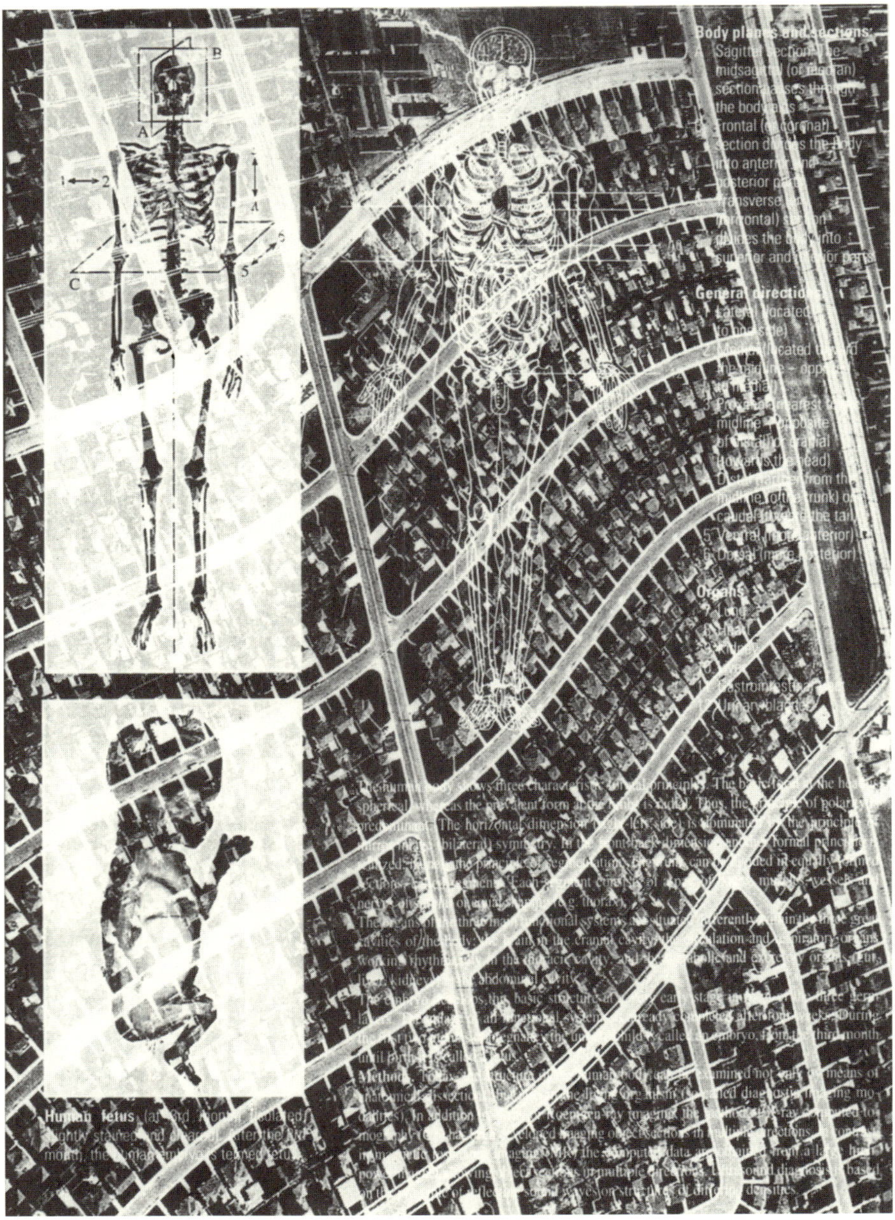

Sarah Nicolai ~ *In Tandem 2*

Acknowledgments

The following people have generously donated money to this issue of
The Healing Muse.
We are deeply grateful for their support.

Sheree Lyn Batson
Karen Blank
Catherine V. Caldicott
Consortium for Culture and Medicine
Wendy Edwards
Anne Marie & Tim Higgins
Anthony Italiano
Margaret Johnston
Barbara Kane
E. Zoe Keeler
Sandra McCabe
Deirdre Neilen
Gloria Neilen
Patricia Numann
Martha Rix
Sharon Ann Snover
Jane & Christopher St. Andrews
Brendan Tapley
Erin Tapley
Joann Tapley
Lynn Tryba
Cindy Wojtecki
Mary Rose Zink

Support *The Healing Muse*

We provide a forum for artistic approaches to the body, illness, and medicine by publishing the voices and perspectives of people with illness and disability, health care practitioners and caregivers.

We need your help!

Support *The Muse* with a contribution of $50 or more and receive a three-year subscription and acknowledgment in the next issue.

Contributor	**$50**
Sponsor	**$100**
Benefactor	**$500**

Send contributions to:

The Healing Muse
SUNY Upstate Medical University
Center for Bioethics and Humanities
725 Irving Ave, Suite 406
Syracuse, NY 13210

Please make checks payable to *The Healing Muse*.

You can also support *The Muse* by ordering a single issue or a discounted three-year subscription. **See the next page for ordering and subscription information.**

Order Your Copies Now!

		Quantity	Amount
The Healing Muse, Volume 7	$10.00	______	$ ______
Individual Back Issues Volumes 1-6 (indicate volume)	$8.00	______	$ ______
Discount Package (Volumes 1-7)	$55.00	______	$ ______
Three-year Subscription (starts with current year)	$28.00	______	$ ______
Educators' Discount on back issues (15+ copies)	$5.00	______	$ ______
Postage: If *outside* U.S., add $3.00/issue	$3.00	______	$ ______
	TOTAL	______	$ ______

Please send a check or money order made out to *The Healing Muse*.

Send orders to:

The Healing Muse
Center for Bioethics and Humanities
SUNY Upstate Medical University
725 Irving Ave., Suite 406
Syracuse, NY 13210

Mail to:

Name ______________________________

Address ______________________________

____

E-mail ______________________________

Day Phone ______________________________

For additional order forms, visit our website at: **www.thehealingmuse.org**

Submission Guidelines & Editorial Policy for *The Healing Muse*

Submissions are collected and juried from September 1st through May 1st. The editors try to respond to submissions within three months' time. The maximum length is 2,500 words (typed double-spaced). Poetry need not be double-spaced.

We recommend that you read excerpts from one or two issues before you submit your manuscript.

You will find these on our website: www.thehealingmuse.org

All submissions should be sent to:

The Healing Muse
Center for Bioethics and Humanities
725 Irving Ave., Suite 406
Syracuse, New York 13210

- Authors are asked to submit hard copy manuscripts and SASE for return of original manuscripts. Please put the word count on the first page. We ask authors whose work is selected for publication to e-mail us their work as an electronic Word file, to note if their prose is *fiction* or non-fiction, and to enclose a three-line (fifty words maximum) bio for our Contributors' page.

- Visual artists should submit clear originals, slides, or electronic files at 300 dpi. Much of the artwork published in *The Healing Muse* is printed in black and white, so please take this into account when submitting your work. All original artwork, slides, photographs, and disks will be returned to the author. Please include SASE with your submission.

- Manuscripts and artworks are considered with the understanding that they have not been published previously in print or electronic format (including the Internet). We ask authors whose work is accepted by *The Healing Muse* to sign a statement declaring that their work has not been previously published by them or under another name. The editors screen submissions carefully for plagiarized texts.

- Accepted manuscripts are edited and returned to authors for approval.

- **Confidentiality**. The privacy of patients and clients of health care practitioners should be protected. Physicians and health care practitioners who write about their patients must alter identifying details and characteristics.

- Contributors will receive two copies of each issue in which their work appears; additional copies are available at a reduced rate.

Questions? Please e-mail us at *The Healing Muse:* **hlgmuse@upstate.edu**

Or visit us at: **http://www.thehealingmuse.org**